FIRST EDITION

Streaming Data Mesh
A Model for Optimizing Real-Time Data Services

Hubert Dulay and Stephen Mooney

Beijing · Boston · Farnham · Sebastopol · Tokyo

Streaming Data Mesh

by Hubert Dulay and Stephen Mooney

Published by O'Reilly Media, Inc., 1005 Gravenstein Highway North, Sebastopol, CA 95472.

O'Reilly books may be purchased for educational, business, or sales promotional use. Online editions are also available for most titles (*http://oreilly.com*). For more information, contact our corporate/institutional sales department: 800-998-9938 or *corporate@oreilly.com*.

Acquisitions Editor: Andy Kwan	**Indexer:** Judith McConville
Development Editor: Jeff Bleiel	**Interior Designer:** David Futato
Production Editor: Beth Kelly	**Cover Designer:** Karen Montgomery
Copyeditor: Sonia Saruba	**Illustrator:** Kate Dullea
Proofreader: Sharon Wilkey	

June 2023:   First Edition

Revision History for the First Edition
2023-05-11:   First Release

See *http://oreilly.com/catalog/errata.csp?isbn=9781098130725* for release details.

978-1-098-13072-5

Table of Contents

Preface

Welcome to this first edition of *Streaming Data Mesh*! This is your guide to understanding and building a streaming data mesh that meets all of the pillars of a data mesh.

Data mesh is one of the most popular architectures for data platforms that many are exploring today. This book will help you get a full understanding of this self-servicing data platform in a streaming context. Today, batch processing dominates all extract, transform, and load (ETL) processes in most businesses. This book will help show a different perspective of data pipelines and apply the same concepts you already understand in batch ETL, but in a streaming ETL in the context of a data mesh.

This book is designed to help you understand the essential concepts around streaming data mesh—the concepts, architectures, and technologies at its core. The book covers all the essential topics related to streaming mesh, from the basics of data architecture, to the use of big data tools for data warehousing, to business-oriented approaches for streaming data mesh architectures. Additionally, we will look at a stack of services involved in a successful streaming data mesh project.

This book does not require you to have preknowledge of the pillars that make up a data mesh. We will briefly introduce the pillars at a very high level and define them with streaming specifically in mind. If you feel you need to understand data mesh in more detail, please refer to Zhamak Dehghani's book, *Data Mesh* (O'Reilly).

Who Should Read This Book

This book is written for anyone who is interested in learning more about streaming data mesh, combining the exciting work done in data mesh with real-time streaming for data transformation, data product definition, and data governance. This book is also useful for data engineers, data analysts, data scientists, software architects, and product owners who want to implement a streaming data architecture for their projects. This book is useful for those who wish to become familiar with streaming data technologies and best practices for integrating them, at scale, into their projects.

Why We Wrote This Book

We wrote a book on streaming data mesh because we believe it has the potential to revolutionize the way companies manage and process their data. Streaming data mesh provides a platform that unites messaging, storage, and processing capabilities into one comprehensive solution. By increasing data reliability and coverage while reducing costs, this platform enables companies to significantly accelerate their digital transformation and become data-driven organizations. With this book, we want to make sure our readers understand the key principles, the latest approaches, and the dos and don'ts of streaming data mesh. We also want to provide step-by-step guidance for setting up and operating a streaming data mesh, taking into account best practices.

Navigating This Book

This book is organized as follows:

- Chapters 1 and 2 provide an introduction to data mesh concepts and extend these into a streaming context.
- Chapter 3 goes into detail about domain ownership and the approaches used to identify domains, domain-driven design, the roles associated with a data domain, tools to consider, as well as an approach to domain-centric charge-backs.
- Chapter 4 explores the creation of streaming data products, including data product identification, ingestion, transformation, and publication.
- Chapter 5 examines federated computational data governance within a streaming data mesh.
- Chapter 6 discusses the self-service infrastructure as it relates to streaming data mesh.
- Chapter 7 dives into the architecture of a streaming data mesh and its components, including infrastructure and cloud architecture.
- Chapter 8 discusses the structure, alignment, and roles associated with building a decentralized team.
- Chapter 9 discusses the application of streaming data mesh for creating feature stores to empower data-science model training and inference.
- Chapter 10 provides a concrete example of creating a streaming data mesh.

Conventions Used in This Book

The following typographical conventions are used in this book:

Italic
> Indicates new terms, URLs, email addresses, filenames, and file extensions.

`Constant width`
> Used for program listings, as well as within paragraphs to refer to program elements such as variable or function names, databases, data types, environment variables, statements, and keywords.

`Constant width bold`
> Shows commands or other text that should be typed literally by the user.

`Constant width italic`
> Shows text that should be replaced with user-supplied values or by values determined by context.

 This element signifies a tip or suggestion.

 This element signifies a general note.

 This element indicates a warning or caution.

Using Code Examples

Supplemental material (code examples, exercises, etc.) is available for download at *https://github.com/hdulay/streaming-data-mesh*.

If you have a technical question or a problem using the code examples, please send email to *support@oreilly.com*.

This book is here to help you get your job done. In general, if example code is offered with this book, you may use it in your programs and documentation. You do not need to contact us for permission unless you're reproducing a significant portion of the code. For example, writing a program that uses several chunks of code from this book does not require permission. Selling or distributing examples from O'Reilly books does require permission. Answering a question by citing this book and quoting example code does not require permission. Incorporating a significant amount of example code from this book into your product's documentation does require permission.

We appreciate, but generally do not require, attribution. An attribution usually includes the title, author, publisher, and ISBN. For example: "*Streaming Data Mesh* by Hubert Dulay and Stephen Mooney (O'Reilly). Copyright 2023 Hubert Dulay and Stephen Mooney, 978-1-098-13072-5."

If you feel your use of code examples falls outside fair use or the permission given above, feel free to contact us at *permissions@oreilly.com*.

O'Reilly Online Learning

 For more than 40 years, *O'Reilly Media* has provided technology and business training, knowledge, and insight to help companies succeed.

Our unique network of experts and innovators share their knowledge and expertise through books, articles, and our online learning platform. O'Reilly's online learning platform gives you on-demand access to live training courses, in-depth learning paths, interactive coding environments, and a vast collection of text and video from O'Reilly and 200+ other publishers. For more information, visit *https://oreilly.com*.

How to Contact Us

Please address comments and questions concerning this book to the publisher:

O'Reilly Media, Inc.
1005 Gravenstein Highway North
Sebastopol, CA 95472
800-889-8969 (in the United States or Canada)
707-829-7019 (international or local)
707-829-0104 (fax)
support@oreilly.com
https://www.oreilly.com/about/contact.html

We have a web page for this book, where we list errata, examples, and any additional information. You can access this page at *https://oreil.ly/streaming-data-mesh*.

For news and information about our books and courses, visit *https://oreilly.com*.

Find us on LinkedIn: *https://linkedin.com/company/oreilly-media*

Follow us on Twitter: *https://twitter.com/oreillymedia*

Watch us on YouTube: *https://youtube.com/oreillymedia*

Acknowledgments

We could not have written this book without Andy Kwan promoting our proposal for it. Thanks also to our production editor, Beth Kelly, and most importantly, Jeff Bleiel. Jeff has been a tremendous help, and we greatly appreciate all that he has done for us.

A special thanks goes out to all of the reviewers who spent countless hours digesting this content and suggesting improvements. Your unwavering support was instrumental to making this book a reality. Ralph Matthias Debusmann, for reaching out and showing his interest early on in our book. Ravneet Singh, thank you too for your help and support. Dr. Ian Buss, thanks again and again! Sharon Xie, Decodable is lucky to have you. Eric Sammer, thanks for the experience.

Hubert

Thanks to my wife, Beth, and kids, Aster and Nico, for supporting me and reminding me to make time for myself and family.

I'd like to specifically thank everyone who influenced me during my time at Cloudera. "Always be building your brand," Hemal Kanani—I still hear your voice when I read that phrase—BOOM! Ben Spivey for always being there as a mentor and friend. Ian Buss for showing me that big data is easy. Marlo Carillo and my filip big data brothers—thanks for representing the RP. And of course, the CLDR Illuminatis.

I'd like to also thank everyone at Confluent who journeyed with me to IPO and for giving me the experiences needed to write this book. Dan Elliman, thanks for being Batman to my Robin in the NE. Eric Langan, thanks for having such a great and contagious attitude. Paul Earsy for guiding me through muddy waters. For Steve Williams: why did you retire? You're still at your prime. Jay Kreps for his leadership. Gwen Shapira for being a huge influence. Yeva Byzek, Ben Stopford, Adam Bellemare, and Travis Hoffman for being there early in the data mesh discourse at Confluent. Thanks, Confluent, for sponsoring this book and for all the other smart people there.

I would also like to thank the many people that provided feedback and helped shape the book: Benjamin Djidi, Ismael Ghalimi, David Yaffe, Hojjat Jafarpour, Yingjun Wu, Zander Matheson, Will Plummer, Ting Wang, Jove Zhong, and Yaniv Ben Hemo.

Stephen

I would like to express my sincere gratitude to everyone who supported me while writing this book. Special thanks to the colleagues who guided me through the process of writing and publishing. I am also grateful to friends and family for their unwavering love and encouragement. Additionally, I am thankful to the editorial team at O'Reilly for their invaluable advice and resources. Finally, I am grateful to the many readers who have been a wonderful source of inspiration for me throughout this journey. Thank you all.

CHAPTER 1

Data Mesh Introduction

Youngsters think that at some point data architectures were easy, and then data volume, velocity, variety grew and we needed new architectures which are hard. In reality, data problems were always organization problems and therefore were never solved.

—Gwen (Chen) Shapira, *Kafka: The Definitive Guide* (O'Reilly)

If you're working at a growing company, you'll realize that a positive correlation exists between company growth and the scale of ingress data. This could be from increased usage for existing applications or newly added applications and features. It's up to the data engineer to organize, optimize, process, govern, and serve this growing data to the consumers while maintaining service-level agreements (SLAs). Most likely, these SLAs were guaranteed to the consumers without the data engineer's input. The first thing you learn when working with such a large amount of data is that when the data processing starts to encroach toward the guarantees made by these SLAs, more focus is put on staying within the SLAs, and things like data governance are marginalized. This in turn generates a lot of distrust in the data being served and ultimately distrust in the analytics—the same analytics that can be used to improve operational applications to generate more revenue or prevent revenue loss.

If you replicate this problem across all lines of business in the enterprise, you start to get very unhappy data engineers trying to speed up data pipelines within the capacity of the data lake and data processing clusters. This is the position where I found myself more often than not.

So what is a data mesh? The term "mesh" in "data mesh" was taken from the term "service mesh," which is a means of adding observability, security, discovery, and reliability at the *platform* level rather than the application layer. A service mesh is typically implemented as a scalable set of network proxies deployed *alongside* application code (a pattern sometimes called a *sidecar*). These proxies handle communication between *microservices* and also act as a point where service mesh features are introduced.

Microservice architecture is at the core of a streaming data mesh architecture, and introduces a fundamental change that decomposes monolithic applications by creating loosely coupled, smaller, highly maintainable, agile, and independently scalable services beyond the capacity of any monolithic architecture. In Figure 1-1 you can see this decomposition of the monolithic application to create a more scalable microservice architecture without losing the business purpose of the application.

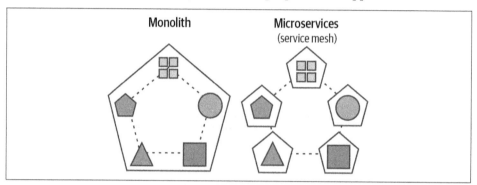

Figure 1-1. Decomposing a monolithic application into microservices that communicate with one another via a service mesh

A data mesh seeks to accomplish the same goals that microservices achieved for monolithic applications. In Figure 1-2 a data mesh tries to create the same loosely coupled, smaller, highly maintainable, agile, and independently scalable *data products* beyond the capacity of any *monolithic data lake* architecture.

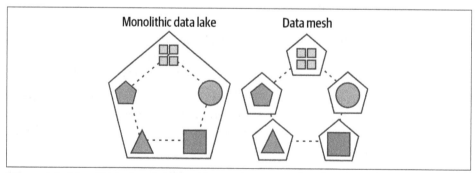

Figure 1-2. Monolithic data lake/warehouse decomposed to data products and domains that communicate via a data mesh

Zhamak Dehghani (whom I refer to as ZD in this book) is the pioneer of the data mesh pattern. If you are not familiar with ZD and her data mesh blog, I highly recommend reading it as well as her very popular book *Data Mesh* (O'Reilly). I will be introducing a simple overview to help you get a basic understanding of the pillars that make up the data mesh architectural pattern so that I can refer to them throughout the book.

In this chapter we will set up the basics of what a data mesh is before we introduce a streaming data mesh in Chapter 2. This will help lay a foundation for better understanding as we overlay ideas of streaming. We will then talk about other architectures that share similarities with data mesh to help delineate them. These other architectures tend to confuse data architects when designing a data mesh, and it is best to get clarity before we introduce data mesh to streaming.

Data Divide

ZD's blog talks about a *data divide*, illustrated in Figure 1-3, to help describe the movement of data within a business. This foundational concept will help in understanding how data drives business decisions and the monolithic issues that come with it.

To summarize, the operational data plane holds data stores that back the applications that power a business.

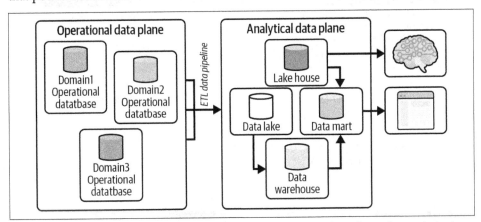

Figure 1-3. The data divide separating the operational data plane from the analytical data plane

An extract, transform, and load (ETL) process replicates the operational data to the analytical data plane, since you do not want to execute analytical queries on operational data stores, taking away compute and storage resources needed to generate revenue for your business. The analytical plane contains data lakes/warehouses/lakehouses to derive insights. These insights are fed back to the operational data plane to make improvements and grow the business.

With the help of Kubernetes on the operational plane, applications have evolved from sluggish and monolithic applications to agile and scalable microservices that inter-communicate, creating a service mesh. The same cannot be said for the analytical plane. The goal of the data mesh is to do just that: to break up the monolithic analytical plane to a decentralized solution to enable agile, scalable, and easie-to-manage data. We will refer to the operational plane and analytical plane throughout the book, so it's important to establish this understanding early as we start to build a streaming data mesh example.

Data Mesh Pillars

The foundation of the data mesh architecture is supported by the pillars defined in Table 1-1. We will quickly summarize them in the following sections, covering the salient concepts of each, so that we can focus on the implementation of a streaming data mesh in later chapters.

Table 1-1. Data mesh pillars defined by ZD

Data ownership	Data as a product	Self-service data platform	Federated computational data governance
Decentralization and distribution of responsibility to people who are closest to the data in order to support continuous change and scalability.	Discovering, understanding, trusting, and ultimately using quality data.	Self-service data infrastructure as a platform to enable domain autonomy.	Governance model that embraces decentralization, domain self-sovereignty, and interoperability through global standardization. A dynamic topology and most importantly automated execution of decisions by the platform.

Data ownership and *data as a product* make up the core of the data mesh pillars. *Self-service data platform* and *federated computational data governance* exist to support the first two pillars. We'll briefly discuss these four now and devote a whole chapter to each pillar beginning with Chapter 3.

Data Ownership

As mentioned previously, the primary pillar of a data mesh is to decentralize the data so that its ownership is given back to the team that originally produced it (or at least know and care about it the most). The data engineers within this team will be assigned a domain—one in which they are experts in the data itself. Some examples of domains are analytics, inventory, and application(s). They are the groups who likely were previously writing to and reading from the monolithic data lake.

Domains are responsible for capturing data from its true source. Each domain transforms, enriches, and ultimately provides that data to its consumers.

There are three types of domains:

Producer only
> Domains that only produce data and don't consume it from other domains

Consumer only
> Domains that only consume data from other domains

Producer and consumer
> Domains that produce and consume data to and from other domains, respectively

 Following the domain-driven design (DDD) approach, which models domain objects defined by the business domain's experts and implemented in software, the domain knows the specific details of its data, such as schema and data types that adhere to these domain objects. Since data is defined at the domain level, it is the best place to define specifics about its definition, transformation, and governance.

Data as a Product

Since data now belongs to a domain, we require a way to serve data between domains. Since this data needs to be consumable and usable, it needs to be treated as any other product so consumers will have a good data experience. From this point forward, we will call any data being served to other domains *data products*.

Defining what a "good experience" is with data products is a task that has to be agreed upon among the domains in the data mesh. An agreed-to definition will help provide well-defined expectations among the participating domains in the mesh. Table 1-2 lists some ideas to think about that will help create a "good experience" for data product consumers and help with building data products in a domain.

Table 1-2. Considerations that can ease the development of data products and create a "good experience" with them

Considerations	Description
Data products should be easily consumable.	Some examples could be: • Cleanliness • Preparedness • High throughput • Interoperability
Engineers should have a generalist skill set.	Engineers need to build data products without needing tools that require hyper-specialized skills. These are a possible minimum set of skills needed to build data products: • SQL • YAML • JSON

Considerations	Description
Data products should be searchable.	When publishing a data product to the data mesh, a data catalog will be used for discovery, metadata views (usage, security, schema, and lineage), and access requests to the data product by domains that may want to consume it.

Federated Computational Data Governance

Since domains are used to create data products, and sharing data products across many domains ultimately builds a mesh of data, we need to ensure that the data being served follows some guidelines. *Data governance* involves creating and adhering to a set of global rules, standards, and policies applied to all data products and their interfaces to ensure a collaborative and interoperable data mesh community. These guidelines must be agreed upon among the participating data mesh domains.

Data mesh is not completely decentralized. The data is decentralized in domains, but the *mesh* part of data mesh is not. Data governance is critical in building the *mesh* in a data mesh. Examples of this include building self-services, defining security, and enforcing interoperability practices.

Here are some things to consider when thinking about data governance for a data mesh: authorization, authentication, data and metadata replication methods, schemas, data serialization, and tokenization/encryption.

Self-Service Data Platform

Because following these pillars requires a set of hyper-specialized skills, a set of services must be created in order to build a data mesh and its data products. These tools require compatibility with skills that are accessible to a more generalist engineer. When building a data mesh, it is necessary to enable existing engineers in a domain to perform the tasks required. Domains have to capture data from their operational stores, transform (join or enrich, aggregate, balance) that data, and publish their data products to the data mesh. Self-service services are the "easy buttons" necessary to make data mesh easy to adopt with high usability. In summary, the self-services enable the domain engineers to take on many of the tasks the data engineer was responsible for across all lines of the business. A data mesh not only breaks up the monolithic data lake, but also breaks up the monolithic role of the data engineer into simple tasks the domain engineers can perform.

We cannot replicate what was done in the data lake to all of the domains. We instead build self-services so that the domains can build a data mesh and publish data products with simple tools and general skills.

Data Mesh Diagram

Figure 1-4 depicts there are three distinct domains: data science, mobile application, and inventory.

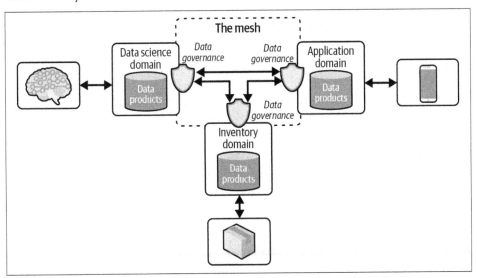

Figure 1-4. High-level view of a data mesh

The *data science domain* consumes data from the application domain, which owns the data coming from mobile applications. The *inventory domain* consumes data from data science for inventory logistics, like reducing distance or moving supply to locations with higher propensity to buy. Lastly, the *application domain* could be consuming references to newly trained models to load into its mobile applications that create updated personalized experiences.

Data governance creates access controls between the data product producer and consumer and provides metadata like schema definitions and lineages. In some cases, mastered data along with reference data may be relevant to the implementation. Data governance allows us to create appropriate access controls for these resources as well.

The edges that connect domains replicate data between them. They build the connections between domains, creating the "mesh." Figure 1-4 is a high-level graph of a data mesh that we will dive deeper into in the following chapters.

In later chapters we will also talk about how to identify and build a domain by assembling a data team that follows the spirit of ZD's vision of a decentralized data platform. Again, Figure 1-4 is a high-level view of a nonstreaming data mesh. Such an implementation does not imply that streaming is the solution for publishing data for consumption. Other alternatives can move data between and within a domain. Chapter 2 covers streaming data mesh specifically and its advantages.

Data Mesh Encompasses Other Meshes Beyond Just Data

You can also think of a data mesh as a way to implement the following features:

Data governance
> To enable interoperability between data governance defined within the domains and to allow domains to define their own governance required by their data products.

Data security
> To enable security between domains and data products. Security includes not just authentication but also authorization via access control lists (ACLs) or role-based access control (RBAC).

Data self-service
> To enable building domains, data products, and domain connections. This could be called *MeshOps* (data mesh operations) to provision and deploy data products and their security.

The streaming data catalog is what brings all these "meshes" together into a single view and extends beyond the scope of a data fabric.

Other Similar Architectural Patterns

The previous section summarized the data mesh architecture at a very high level as defined by ZD's vision. Many data architects like to point out existing data architectures that have similar characteristics to a data mesh. These similarities may be enough for architects to label their existing implementations as already conforming to and meeting the data mesh pillars. These architects may be absolutely correct or partially correct. A few of these data architectures include data fabrics, data gateways, data as a service, data democratization, and data virtualization.

Data Fabric

A *data fabric* is a pattern that is very similar to a data mesh in that both provide solutions encompassing data governance and self-service: discovery, access, security, integration, transformation, and lineage (Figure 1-5).

At the time of this writing, consensus on the differences between data mesh and data fabric is unclear. In simple terms, a *data fabric* is a metadriven means of connecting disparate sets of data and related tools to provide a cohesive data experience and to deliver data in a self-service manner.

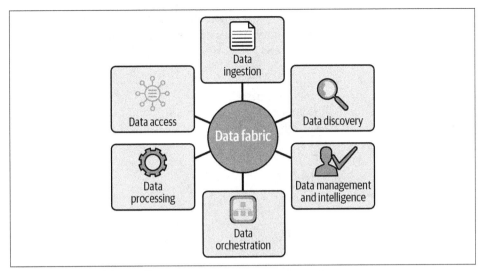

Figure 1-5. Data fabric pillars

While a data mesh seeks to solve many of the same problems that a data fabric addresses—namely, the ability to address data in a single, composite data environment—the approach is different. While a data fabric enables users to create a single, virtual layer on top of distributed data, a data mesh further empowers distributed groups of data producers to manage and publish data as they see fit. Data fabrics allow for a low-to-no-code data virtualization experience by applying data integration within APIs that reside within the data fabric. The data mesh, however, allows for data engineers to write code for APIs with which to interface further.

A data fabric is an architectural approach to provide data access across multiple technologies and platforms, and is based on a technology solution. One key contrast is that a data mesh is much more than just technology: it is a pattern that involves people and processes. Instead of taking ownership of an entire data platform, as in a data fabric, the data mesh allows data producers to focus on data production, allows data consumers to focus on consumption, and allows hybrid teams to consume other data products, blend other data to create even more interesting data products, and publish these data products—with some data governance considerations in place.

In a data mesh, data is decentralized, while in a data fabric, centralization of data is allowed. And with data centralization like data lakes, you get the monolithic problems that come with it. Data mesh tries to apply a microservices approach to data by decomposing data domains into smaller and more agile groups.

Fortunately, the tools that support a data fabric can support a data mesh. It's also apparent that a data mesh will need additional self-services that support the domains in engineering data products and provision the infrastructure to build and serve data products. In Figure 1-6 we see that a data mesh has all the components of a data fabric but implemented in a mesh. Simply put, a data fabric is a subset of a data mesh.

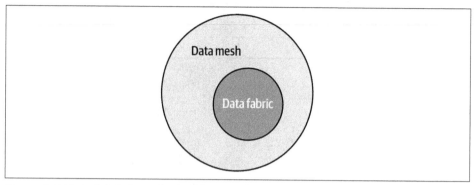

Figure 1-6. Data fabric is a subset of data mesh

Data Gateways and Data Services

Data gateways are like API gateways but serve data:

> Data gateways act like API gateways but focusing on the data aspect. A data gateway offers abstractions, security, scaling, federation, and contract-driven development features.
>
> —Bilgin Ibryam, "Data Gateways in the Cloud Native Era" from *InfoQ*, May 2020

Similarly, *data as a service* (*DaaS*) is a pattern that serves data from its original source that is fully managed and consumable by following open standards and is *served by software as a service* (*SaaS*). Both architectural patterns serve data, but DaaS is focused more on serving the data from the cloud. You could say that DaaS enables data gateways in the cloud, where it previously may have been on only premises. Figure 1-7 shows an example.

Combining the concepts of both data gateways and DaaS, it is easier to qualify data as *coming from the original source*, especially if the data was immutable from the source. Replication of data that originated from an on-premises data center to a SaaS in the cloud would be a requirement.

All the requirements for DaaS are satisfied by data mesh except for being enabled by a SaaS. In data mesh, SaaS is an option, but currently there are no SaaS data mesh providers that make implementing a data mesh easy.

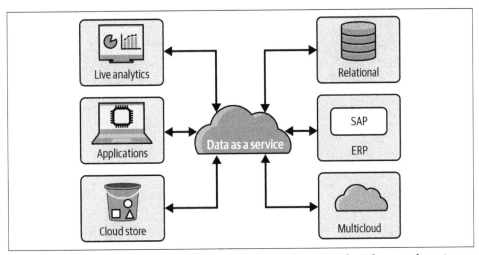

Figure 1-7. Data as a service (DaaS) has a similar goal as providing data products in a data mesh

Data Democratization

Data democratization is the process of making digital information accessible to the average nontechnical user of information systems without having to require the involvement of IT:

> Data democratization means that everybody has access to data and there are no gatekeepers that create a bottleneck at the gateway to the data. It requires that we accompany the access with an easy way for people to understand the data so that they can use it to expedite decision-making and uncover opportunities for an organization. The goal is to have anybody use data at any time to make decisions with no barriers to access or understanding.
>
> —Bernard Marr, "What Is Data Democratization? A Super Simple Explanation and the Key Pros and Cons," *Forbes*, July 2017

Data mesh satisfies this definition through its data products, self-service, and low-code approach to sharing and creating data. Simple access to data is critical in keeping a business data driven. Getting fast access to data to create analytical insights will enable faster response to operational changes that could save a business from high costs.

Data Virtualization

Data virtualization is a special kind of data integration technology that provides access to real-time data, across multiple sources and extremely large volumes, without having to move any data to a new location.[1]

Many have considered data virtualization as a solution to implementing a data mesh since it can satisfy all the pillars of a data mesh architecture, especially the idea of not having to move any data to a new location, which requires replication of the data using a separate ETL process. As we start to talk about streaming data mesh, we need to understand the difference between data virtualization and data replication, which is the approach a streaming data mesh takes.

As stated before, with data virtualization, the data isn't moved to a new location and therefore is not copied multiple times when performing queries, unlike data replication. Depending on how far the data is spread out, this may be beneficial. However, if data exists in multiple global regions, performing queries across long distances will affect query performance significantly. The purpose of replicating data from operational to analytical planes using ETL is to not only prevent ad hoc queries from being executed on the operational data stores, which would affect the operational applications powering the business; but also bring the data closer to the tools performing the analytics. So ETL is still needed, and replication is inevitable:

> Data virtualization comes from a world-view where data storage is expensive and networking is cheap (i.e., on premise). The problem it solved is making the data accessible no matter where it is and without having to copy it. Copies in databases are bad because of the difficulty in guaranteeing consistency. Data replication is based on the view that copies aren't bad (because the data has been mutated). Which turns out to be more useful when it's the network that's expensive (the cloud).
>
> —Mic Hussey, principal solutions engineer at Confluent

Consider a hybrid replication and virtualization. As the data starts to reside in different global regions, it could be better to replicate the data to a region and then implement data virtualization within a region.

Focusing on Implementation

Streaming is not a requirement in ZD's definition of a data mesh. Serving data products in a data mesh can be implemented as batching or streaming APIs. ZD also states that data mesh should be used for only analytical use cases. We will take data mesh beyond analytical and apply it to architectures that provide solutions for DaaS

---

1 Kriptos; "What is Data Virtualization? Understanding the Concept and its Advantages," *Data Virtualization*, February 2022.

and data fabrics. Chapter 2 highlights some of the advantages for streaming over batching data mesh.

Taking the fundamentals of data mesh and applying them to a streaming context will require us to make implementation choices so that we can build a streaming data mesh by example. The implementation choices made within this book are not necessarily requirements for a streaming data mesh but options chosen to help stitch the streaming solution together while adhering to ZD's data mesh pillars. The two key technologies required for a streaming implementation will require (1) a streaming technology such as Apache Kafka, Redpanda, or Amazon Kinesis; and (2) a way to expose data as asynchronous resources, using a technology such as AsyncAPI. As this book progresses, we will focus on implementations using Kafka and AsyncAPI.

Apache Kafka

Apache Kafka as the implementation for streaming data platforms. This book doesn't require you to know Apache Kafka but will cover just the important features that enable a proper streaming data mesh. Also, Kafka can be replaced with a similar streaming platform like Apache Pulsar or Redpanda, both of which follow the Apache Kafka producer and consumer framework. It is important to note that streaming platforms that are able to keep their data in a *commit log* will best implement the streaming data mesh pattern described in this book. Commit logs in a streaming platform are described in Chapter 2.

AsyncAPI

AsyncAPI is an open source project that simplifies asynchronous event-driven architecture (EDA). AsyncAPI is a framework that allows implementors to generate code or configurations, in whichever language or tool like, to produce or consume streaming data. It allows you to describe any streaming data in an AsyncAPI configuration in a simple, descriptive, and interoperable way. It will be one of the foundational components we'll use to build a streaming data mesh. AsyncAPI alone is not enough to define data products in a streaming data mesh. However, since AsyncAPI is extensible, we will extend it to include the data mesh pillars previously defined. We will go over the details of AsyncAPI in later chapters.

With the data mesh and its defined pillars, let's take a deeper look into how we can apply the pillars and concepts discussed in this chapter to streaming data to create a streaming data mesh.

CHAPTER 2

Streaming Data Mesh Introduction

In Chapter 1 we introduced and summarized all four pillars of a data mesh architecture. Now we will apply that introductory knowledge to a streaming data mesh. Simply put, a *streaming data mesh* is a data mesh (with all its pillars satisfied) that is implemented as streams. In other words, after data is ingested from the source, there isn't any point where that data is rested into a data store before reaching the consuming domain. Data products are kept in a stream until their retention expires.

Keeping data products in a stream requires all the self-service tools and services available to the data mesh. Consider a simple ETL process. The component that extracts data from the source needs to set the data in motion in a stream. Next, the engine that transforms the data needs to transform it in a stream. Lastly, the component that publishes the data product needs to support integrations so consumers can easily stream the data product into their own domain while following the federated computational data governance for streaming data products. Table 2-1 shows the four data mesh pillars and explains what happens in a streaming setting.

Table 2-1. The data mesh pillars in the context of a streaming data mesh

Streaming data mesh pillar	Description
Data ownership (domain ownership)	The domain sets its data products in motion as streams.
Data as a product (data product)	Domains are responsible for transforming data into discoverable and trustable high-quality streaming data products.
Self-serve data platform (self-services)	The self-service data platform enables domains to stream data from the source to the consuming domain while maintaining autonomy.
Federated computational data governance (streaming data governance)	A streaming data governance model that embraces decentralization, domain self-sovereignty, and interoperability through global standardization for streaming data.

For consistency, we will refer to data ownership as *domain owner-ship*, data as a product as *data product*, self-serve data platform as *self-services*, and federated computational data governance as simply *data governance*. We will assume that all these terms imply streaming data, also called *data in motion*.

In this chapter we will discuss the advantages of stream processing over batch processing when implementing a data mesh. We will also introduce the Kappa architecture and how it enables these advantages.

The Streaming Advantage

Streaming data mesh comes with a few advantages over batch processing that usually don't manifest until you build your first use case. These advantages exist in both the technical implementation and business outcomes.

Streaming Enables Real-Time Use Cases

The first advantage of streaming data mesh is that it enables data-consuming domains to handle true real-time use cases. Streaming is the only means of accomplishing true real-time capabilities in a data product. If the data pipeline stores the data at any time while replicating it from the operational plane to the consuming domain, then we've taken away all potential consuming domains' real-time capabilities. When you store data at any point in the pipeline, you will force your data pipeline to have batch semantics that include the use of a CRON-like tool to schedule a read, or set of reads, from the data store.

Even if existing domains do not currently have any real-time use cases, *streaming supports both batch use cases and real-time use cases*. It makes more sense to implement your data pipelines as streaming initially. Otherwise, not implementing a data mesh as real-time streams could result in a very large technical debt that would be difficult to pay back. As a business grows, the more data-driven it becomes, and requests for quick analytical insights will increase. We should anticipate real-time use cases even if we don't have any today.

Streaming data sets a new standard for data processing and AI. Time delays created with batch processing have made enterprises slow to react to business needs. This becomes an even more critical issue when insights obtained from an analytical model inference become delayed because of batch processing, further resulting in revenue loss or the potential dissatisfaction of customers being served. Additionally, underlying data for a model changes rapidly. Training an analytical model from a stale data source creates a possibility of inferring (scoring) data against a model that no longer represents the data being inferred. This discrepancy in data, commonly referred to as *training-serving skew*, becomes a challenging problem for model stability, as changes in data when you serve are not accurately accounted for when a model is trained. One key motivation for considering a streaming architecture is to minimize training-serving skew.

Streaming Enables Data Optimization Advantages

When you extract data from an operational store, that data is put in motion. By putting it into a streaming platform like Apache Kafka, the data is kept in motion and is automatically optimized by partitioning and indexing, thus making producing and consuming very efficient. If you take your data out of the stream and put it at rest in a data store, you're forced to re-optimize your data by partitioning, indexing, bucketing, or compacting it so that any downstream process can consume it efficiently from the data store. This begs the question as to why you put data in the data store to begin with if data processing has not finished.

Figure 2-1 shows what happens when data is removed from the streaming layer and placed into a data lake. Real-time data that is taken out of the stream will almost always create small files in the data lake, because data is streamed per event.

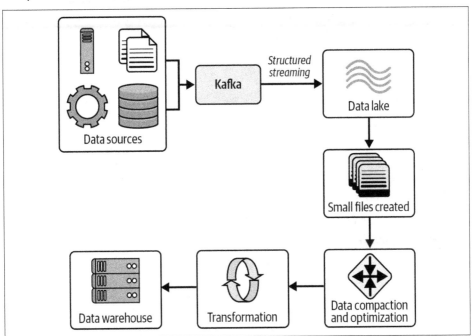

Figure 2-1. When you consume data from data sources, send it to Apache Kafka, and store it straight into a data lake, moving data out of the stream requires you to re-optimize data for downstream consumption by compacting it before it can be processed

These events create smaller files on the cluster, as opposed to creating larger files that are bulk uploaded (*bulk uploading* is a batch processing characteristic and does not provide real-time capabilities). *Small files are a data processing killer.* Aside from suboptimal block usage issues, this pattern has a plethora of downsides:

- These small files force the data lake to keep track of more metadata per file, causing performance degradation and eventually out-of-memory (OOM) issues.
- If the data lake is a cloud store, the overwhelming number of API calls being made for data and metadata can boost cloud costs tenfold.
- The data processing engine also suffers by slowing query performance since it has to manage more metadata per file.
- The parallel tasks in the processing engine are skewed, causing only a few of the tasks to process most of the data.

It's a painful problem to have. The solution is to add a *data compaction and optimization* step to merge all the small files into larger files. This extra step creates fewer files, as shown in the next step, after the small files are created in Figure 2-1. The downstream steps eventually reach the destination in the data warehouse. Adding a data compaction step ultimately increases data latency, which moves us further away from the goal of a real-time data processing architecture. As a result, training-serving skew increases and performance suffers.

Reverse ETL

Extract, transform, and load (ETL) is a process of moving data from a source to a destination, often used to move data from the operational plane to the analytical plane. The movement of data is akin to water flowing downstream to a lake. All the technical systems involved in the ETL process support a natural flow to the lake because that's what they were built and optimized for.

Conversely, *reverse ETL (rETL)* moves data in the opposite direction: from the analytical plane to the operational plane. Companies do this because the core definitions of their business live only in the data warehouse, and the operational applications need this core definition:

> Putting high-priced analytical database systems in the hot path introduces pants-on-head anti-patterns to supportability and ops. Who can say with a straight face that putting a data warehouse between two tier 1 apps is a good idea? Not many shops treat analytical systems—the data warehouse, ELT systems, offline feature stores, visualization systems—like tier 1, business-critical components.
>
> —Eric Sammer, "We're Abusing The Data Warehouse; rETL, ELT, And Other Weird Stuff," *Decodable*, May 2022

rETL is also known as *data activation*.

The problem with rETL is that it is an unnatural flow of data. You're literally moving against the current by moving data that was in the analytical plain upstream. Systems that support plain ETL are being used to do rETL. But those systems like to move data downstream, not upstream. For example, the data warehouse is not optimized for reads like an operational database. It's optimized for analytics and used to find insights for business decision makers, not users of a customer-facing application.

This is where a streaming data mesh really has an advantage. If the data in the data warehouse is already in a streaming platform, it's easily consumable by the operational plane to serve to customer-facing applications. The metaphor of a "mesh" is a lot different from a unidirectional "flow" of data to a data warehouse or lake. In a mesh, every direction is allowed.

The Kappa Architecture

Before we talk about the Kappa architecture, we need to first understand its predecessor, the Lambda architecture. This pattern was first introduced in *Big Data* by Nathan Marz and James Warren (Manning). The goal was to provide real-time use cases atop a big data system.

Lambda Architecture Introduction

The *Lambda architecture* is a data pipeline that has two branches: real-time streaming and batch (see Figure 2-2).

The two branches could also be referred to as "online" for the streaming branch and "offline" for the batch branch. This is because the batch branch requires a data store that can hold historical data (most likely a data warehouse or data lake). The real-time, or speed, branch requires an in-memory store. To understand better which data stores to choose, it's best to follow the CAP theorem in Figure 2-3.

For the *batch* branch in a Lambda architecture, a data store that supports *partition tolerance* is used to enable horizontal scalability, allowing for storage of large amounts of historical data. As you add more data, partitions and nodes can be added to automatically increase capacity in both compute and storage in the data store. Of the other two CAP features, *availability* is more important than consistency for the batch branch. This is because consistency is already handled by the *streaming* branch.

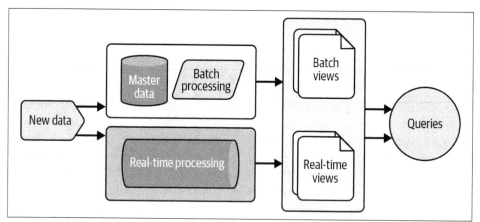

Figure 2-2. Lambda architecture has both a batch processing layer and a real-time (or streaming) processing layer

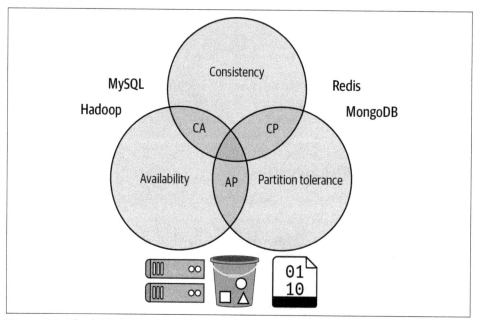

Figure 2-3. The CAP theorem models consistency, availability, and partitionability (or partition tolerance); data stores can provide only two of the three capabilities

When you have a highly available data store (Availability in Figure 2-3), better data resiliency is achieved since partition tolerance on a batch source requires multiple copies of data. In most common use cases, three copies is the standard, allowing up to two copies of data to become unavailable without losing a batch data source. With both availability and partition tolerance (AP), a data store can be created that can hold large amounts of historical data without losing any of it to a partial outage.

CAP Theorem

Dr. Eric Brewer formulated the CAP theorem about distributed network applications in the late 1990s:

C *(Consistency)*
> All reads receive the most recent write or an error.

A *(Availability)*
> All reads receive data without error, but also without the guarantee that it contains the most recent write.

P *(Partition tolerance)*
> The system continues to operate despite an arbitrary number of messages being dropped (or delayed) by the network between nodes.

For the *streaming* branch, a data store that supports *consistency* is more important since it should hold the latest states of the data. If there are different states of the data between partitions of the data store, the real-time states cannot be determined. What the real-time/online data store is responsible for in a Lambda architecture is building a real-time view. See the historical events as key-value pairs in Table 2-2 and the real-time view in Table 2-3.

Table 2-2. Historical events in the batch branch of a Lambda architecture (may not have all the events because the batch process may not have run yet)

Key	Value	Timestamp
1	bar	2022-09-25 17:45:30.005
1	foo	2022-09-25 17:46:45.010
2	streaming	2022-09-25 17:46:47.020

Table 2-3. Real-time view in the streaming branch (may not have all the events because it may hold data for only 24 hours)

Key	Value	Timestamp
1	bar	2022-09-25 17:45:30.005
3	data mesh	2022-09-25 17:46:48.010

Notice that the historical data (populated by the batch branch) and the real-time view (populated by the streaming branch) are not consistent. In the *historical events* in Table 2-2, key 3 is missing because the batch process has not yet finished or started to populate it into the historical offline store. When the batch starts, key 3 will eventually make it into Table 2-2. It also has both versions of key 1 because this is the historical data store.

In the *real-time view* in Table 2-3, key 2 is missing because it was added 24 hours earlier and no longer exists in the online data store. It also has key 3 because it only recently arrived and will automatically appear in the online store.

A *materialized view* is perpetually updating, whereas a *plain view* runs when the query is executed. This is the view that encapsulates the latest state of every key-value pair. For instance, if the record whose key = 1 and value is "foo" is sent to the data store, while subsequently another record whose key = 1 and value is "bar" is immediately sent, the record in the materialized view will be key = 1 and value is "bar", essentially the latest value of the key. At the end of the Lambda pipeline, you will need to synchronize the streaming and batch data stores together to get a real-time historical view of the data. This synchronization becomes tricky when you're trying to join two distinct data stores. Most likely the synchronization would be written in Python or a JVM-based language. The final synchronized table will look like Table 2-4.

Table 2-4. Synchronized view of historical and real-time event

Key	Value
1	bar
2	streaming
3	data mesh

The batch branch of a Lambda architecture suffers greatly from the limitations that small files create. A data optimization step is always needed to ensure that the data is balanced across parallel processes; otherwise, a majority of the data could be going through only a few processes, which will make the data pipeline take a lot longer. The data compaction and optimization step will start to encroach on the SLAs made with consumers as the data grows. If these consumers are paying customers, these optimization issues will start to immediately affect the business.

In a Kappa architecture, data balance must be considered at the beginning of the data pipeline. Maintaining that balance keeps the data optimized throughout the data pipeline until its destination. This will allow you to omit the *data compaction and optimization*—a step that can take minutes, even hours, to complete.

Kappa Architecture Introduction

The *Kappa architecture* is a simplification of the Lambda architecture and allows you to have only a streaming pipeline as your data source. In the Lambda architecture, the historical data was obtained from the batch pipeline, which reads data from a data lake or warehouse. So if a Kappa architecture has only the streaming pipeline, where does the historical data come from? In Kappa architecture, the streaming platform will need the ability to return historical data to its consumer. To do this, it has to either scale out its storage by adding more brokers in the streaming platform cluster, or enable tiered storage capabilities, by offloading older data into a lower tier outside of the brokers in the streaming platform. Tiered storage is the recommended choice because it removes the requirement for scaling out the streaming platform by adding more brokers, which would end up being costly.

By not using tiered storage, a streaming platform will continually require horizontal scaling activities in order to hold all historical data—an expense that also requires all the features of top-tier storage for all data across time. Horizontal scaling in this manner also adds compute capacity to the cluster that it doesn't necessarily need. Scaling out requires more additional partitions and brokers to the streaming platform as well as more commit logs (or partitions), this allowing data to be spread throughout the cluster.

Tiered storage provides a simpler and cheaper way of holding historical data, but it forces a change in the way the streaming platform interfaces with its consumers by allowing them to request historical data and not just the latest data like the traditional messaging systems. This change illustrates the concept of *event-driven* versus *event sourcing*.

Kappa architecture requires a streaming platform that allows for event sourcing, and not just event-driven architecture, to enable you to retrieve the historical data. In the event-driven architecture (EDA) pattern, services subscribe to events, or changes, in state. The subscribing service acts on the event change. An example is a *person* changing their status from *single* to *married*. The service subscribed to this state change may send out payroll and benefit changes to Human Resources.

The basic difference is this: the streaming platform can hold its data in a commit log infinitely. A commit log is a data structure used by Apache Kafka. New data is always appended at the end of the log and is immutable (see Figure 2-4).

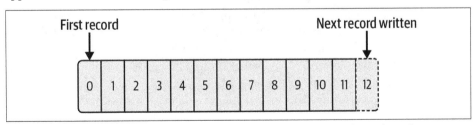

Figure 2-4. Apache Kafka commit log—new data is appended at the end, and every record is assigned an offset

A subset of EDA is *event sourcing*, illustrated in Figure 2-5. EDAs typically are built upon messaging systems. Some traditional messaging systems that support only EDAs are IBM MQ, RabbitMQ, ActiveMQ, Kinesis, Google Pub/Sub, and others. All these messaging systems enable EDA.

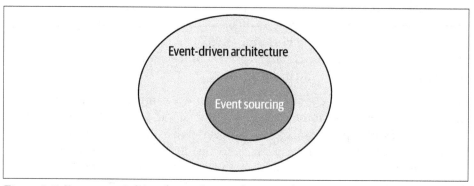

Figure 2-5. Event sourcing is a form of event-driven architecture

The commit log can be configured to retain its data, which provides the ability to perform stateful joins and aggregations between other commit logs in the streaming platform. Previously, these stateful transformations could be done only in a database; this means putting your data at rest which will force batch processing semantics.

Also note that large historical joins in a relational context often present many problems in terms of performance and scalability. Often, these relationships require multiple writes and reads from disk in order to satisfy the query output. Streaming, on the other hand, allows the user or developer to intersect data within the stream at the relevant point in time.

To achieve a streaming data mesh, it's important to keep your data in motion. Doing so will avoid the extra data optimization steps required when writing it to a data store. This will allow you to perform real-time, stateful transformations (joins and aggregations) without having to first rest your events in a database.

Every record in the data is assigned an offset so that data consumers can remember where they stopped consuming or replay records from a specific offset. When infinite storage is enabled, this commit log will go on infinitely. In Apache Kafka, streaming data is held in topics, which are made up of commit logs. The commit logs serve as a way to partition data to enable parallelization in data processing. In this book, the term "commit log" is synonymous with "partition" in the context of Apache Kafka. If tiered storage is used, the streaming platform will mark a record as being in the *cold-set* (data that is older and not accessed often) and will migrate it to a lower tier, keeping the *hot-set* data (data that is newer and needs to be quickly accessed) in the faster top tier.

As of this writing, tiered storage implementation in Apache Kafka is still in progress and is labeled under KIP-405 (Kafka Improvement Proposals). Other similar streaming platforms like Redpanda and Apache Pulsar already have tiered storage implemented in their brokers. Confluent Platform also has tiered storage already implemented with a purchase of an enterprise license.

In Figure 2-6 we see how tiered storage is implemented in the Confluent server. The lower storage tier is an object storei—.e., Amazon S3, Google Cloud Storage, Azure Blob Store. The top tier is storage within the Kafka brokers. When applications request data that is outside the hot-set, Confluent servers reach into the object store to pull the requested data and serve it back to the application.

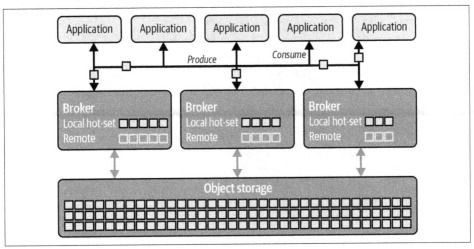

Figure 2-6. Confluent server tiered storage implementation

Summary

The advantages of a streaming data mesh should be motivating for data product engineers and data product consumers. For example, the data engineer will no longer have to maintain two data pipelines in the Lambda architecture, no longer have worry about small file issues in the data lake, and finally build data pipelines that more consistently meet SLAs. The data product consumer is no longer limited to batch-only use cases and can react faster to the business and better serve them. In the next chapters we will talk about how we can build a streaming data mesh by first building domains.

CHAPTER 3

Domain Ownership

The first of the four pillars of a streaming data mesh that we will discuss is domain ownership. Defining a data domain can be difficult, especially when data is often shared with multiple domains, or when a domain has a dependency on data from another domain.

However, at its core, data domains are quite simple to define. *Domains* are the people and systems involved in generating data that is logically grouped. A domain refers to an area of interrelated data pertaining to a common purpose, object, or concept. This data will eventually get shared (and potentially transformed) into published data products. Data domains also have output ports that define how data products will be shared and input ports that define how data is consumed from other domains (see Figure 3-1).

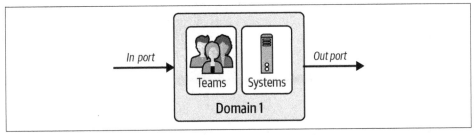

Figure 3-1. A data mesh domain can have many input and output ports

These ports build the interconnections between domains that create the data mesh. The ports represent the production and consumption of data products. In a streaming data mesh, these ports are streaming data products.

The systems and teams internal to the domain do not get exposed to the mesh. They do help support the management and development of the streaming data products. In this chapter we will outline ways to identify domains to ensure that the domain will operate seamlessly in the streaming data mesh.

Identifying Domains

Figure 3-1 shows that teams and systems are contained in a domain and therefore can influence its definition. Teams influence the definition by being experts in their business domain and the applications they maintain and develop. Systems influence the definition because of their physical locations and the data they hold. Teams and systems cluster together to work as one unit to create streaming data products.

It's significant to understand that factors affecting the production of data products influence the identification of a domain more so than factors that affect consuming data products. Consuming domains only expect assurance in the data product, while producers own the work to provide that assurance. We will discuss some of these factors throughout the book.

A reoccurring analogy we use in this book to help you better understand this is *shopping for produce in a grocery store*. As a shopper, you want to inspect your produce before purchasing and eventually consuming it. Seeing that it's protected from the elements assures shoppers of its cleanliness. For example, seeing an organic label may provide consumers with a sense of confidence that their food product is of high quality. It takes a lot of effort for farmers and distributors to convey that sense of assurance and quality for their products.

Discernible Domains

It is easy to identify domains based on *source-aligned* data. You simply create a domain wherever the data originates or is produced. Things that use and understand the data tend to assemble around that data. This includes applications, engineers, and business experts who are tasked to solve business problems. Likewise, it is easy to identify domains based on *application team or business problem*. You simply create a domain where teams are solving a business problem.

Geographic Regions

Teams that are separated by large geographical distances requiring asynchronous communication such as email and Slack make it difficult to keep data in a single domain. The long distance not only makes team communication strenuous, but also creates the potential for a slow data product. Thus, identifying domains by geographic region may be worthwhile in these situations.

Figure 3-2 shows a simple data pipeline that takes data from two sources, joins them, and publishes the resulting data product to the data mesh. If any of the arrows require spanning over distant geographical regions, the pipeline may run too slowly to meet the SLA expectations of data product consumers. The pipeline will also experience some ill effects because many of the tools used to process data aren't meant to be stretched such far distances.

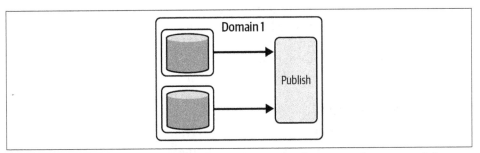

Figure 3-2. Simple pipeline that ingests data from a database, transforms it, and then publishes the data to the data mesh

In this scenario, if one of the sources resides in a remote region, it would be beneficial to create a new domain for it and have it publish a data product for the current domain.

In Figure 3-3, the ingestion from the source database is performed by a new domain (Domain 2). Domain 2 then publishes the data product to the data mesh. The original domain (Domain 1) is now a consumer of the data product(s) from Domain 2, and performs its transformations prior to publishing its own data product. This separation of the original domain forces Domain 2 to provide a data product that meets the SLA requirements of Domain 1.

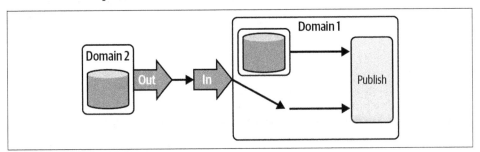

Figure 3-3. In this pipeline, the source is in another region, so a separate domain (2) is created and shares its data through the data mesh with Domain 1

So how does Domain 2 provide a better SLA since it still needs to provide its data to Domain 1 from a far distance? The solution would be for Domain 2 to replicate its data products across the long distance so that the data product is provided locally to Domain 1 without needing to stretch its data pipeline. The replication of the data product is unnoticed and unknown by Domain 1, and the data remains in motion and in real time. The details for this pattern will be discussed in Chapter 7.

Consuming another domain's data products to enhance data products within another domain can easily be misinterpreted as a subdomain. There is, however, a difference. In the previous example, we are treating Domain 2 as a first-class domain, with its data product(s) maintained by a dat-dedicated team that understands the business context of the data and is able to deliver high-quality, reliable data products that are transformed and ready for consumption by other domains. Subdomains take on a more hierarchical approach in controlling the publishing of facets within a domain. While the two approaches are similar, there is a distinction.

Subdomains and subdata mesh

Nothing in the pillars of the data mesh architecture prohibits us from creating subdomains in a larger domain. But in the data mesh, subdomains should appear as regular top domains. The domain-subdomain hierarchy is just metadata that will serve as additional information to data product consumers as they decide on using a data product. We can also use some creative means to take advantage of inheritance and relationships between the domain and subdomain. This presents opportunities in creating more manageable self-service tools, at the cost of complexities in implementation.

Creating a *subdata mesh*, a data mesh that exists within a domain, similarly may also be too complex to implement. The amount of metadata that will be needed to keep a data mesh separate from others might be too much to manage. It may be easier and more elegant to keep domains and their products flat, allowing for easier discoverability and searchability. Domains can still exist within a single umbrella-like structure, yet it may be more feasible to serve subdomain pattern data as metadata to the domain. This allows some subdomain data (not all) to be served as informational only, and would become part of the description of a data product.

Data sovereignty

Being in multiple geographical regions will require specific knowledge of data sovereignty regulations in each region (such as GDPR). These rules enforce regulation as to where private data physically resides and is being sent, along with how it is used. *Data sovereignty* is about protecting sensitive, private data and ensuring it remains under the control of its owner. Data sovereignty rules are country specific, so capturing the location of where data originated is also critical in the lineage of each data point.

Within the context of a data mesh, reasons for splitting domains that span across multiple regions are not only technical but also legal. A full understanding of governance rules specific to a region is critical in avoiding large fines. In many cases, these fines may apply to every record of a violation within the entire data set that was affected, not just the records exposed. For a single domain, understanding multiple data sovereignty rules could be overwhelming and difficult to implement. Separating the domains by their data sovereignty rules gets you on the path to thinking about data governance before any data is shared in the data mesh.

When governance comes first, rule sets can be imposed in code immediately instead of retroactively, which is clearly risky. Some things to start considering early in the development of a domain include how to encrypt, tokenize, obfuscate, or filter out data while still allowing for data democratization within the rules of data sovereignty. As users become more clever in how to abuse data resources, it can be expected that data sovereignty rules will change. Implementation of rules needs to be agile, flexible, and easily deployable so that requirements can be changed without involving significant code changes and large deployments. Also understand that data sovereignty rules may affect only a few attributes or fields within the entire data set. Having the ability to identify or annotate those private attributes in the metadata layer of the data set would make implementations of data sovereignty rules more configurable and adept to changes. More details of how to implement security and governance will be discussed in later chapters.

Hybrid Architecture

Hybrid architectures do not follow the same logic as geographical distance in the previous section, since on-premises systems may have different security requirements than cloud-based ones. It may not be feasible, or even possible, to expose public endpoints for on-premises data products for other domains to consume. In this case, if a domain has systems that live both on premises and in a cloud provider, it may be better to keep all data resources within the same domain and hide the complex and secured network topology from consumers of the data products.

In Figure 3-4, both cloud and on-premises data centers are in one domain. Data from the source database on premises is replicated to the cloud, enriched with another data source in the cloud, then exposed as a data product. Consumers see only the final data product. Not only is the data replicated but the metadata is as well, preserving lineage. If an on-premises domain doesn't have any cloud infrastructure, it may be beneficial to create one to enable data access to more data consumers.

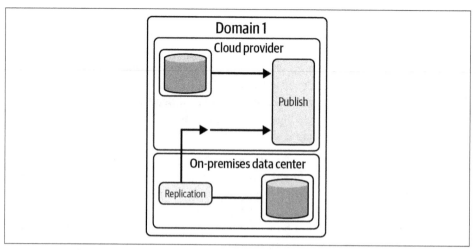

Figure 3-4. A hybrid data pipeline that replicates data from on premises to the cloud provider and publishes a data product

Multicloud

Spanning the business across multiple cloud providers allows for high resiliency to outages involving any single cloud provider. This obviously gives a lot more confidence and assurance to paying customers. It's also a cost benefit to your customers to provide services in their cloud of choice, which will allow them to not accrue costs related to network egress (more detail surrounding costs and charge-back will be covered later in this chapter).

Replication of data again comes into play. Similarly to replicating across geographical regions, data would be replicated across cloud providers. This could be done within a single domain or as separate domains, depending on the use case. There are several ways to accomplish this, which we will discuss in later chapters.

Disaster recovery

If the reason for a multicloud solution is for disaster recovery (DR) from a single cloud provider, it would be more appropriate to keep both sides of the data replication within the same domain to keep the tasks related to DR within the domain. The solution (or application) that spans cloud providers would most likely be set up as active-passive or active-active, as shown in Figures 3-5 and 3-6.

Figure 3-5 depicts two operational databases in two different cloud service providers (CSPs). Operational data is replicated from CSP1 to CSP2 to keep the state of the applications in CSP2 in case of a disaster in CSP1. This is an *active-passive* DR solution: the active state is CSP1, and the disaster/passive state is CPS2. This solution does not utilize all the resources of CSP2 because of its passive state. CSP2 gets utilized fully only when the applications fail over to it because of an outage in CPS1.

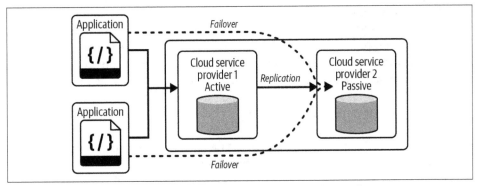

Figure 3-5. An active-passive DR solution for multiple cloud providers

The *active-active* DR solution in Figure 3-6 utilizes the resources of both CSPs. Only the applications using the failed cloud provider fail over to the other CSP, as opposed to all the applications in the active-passive solution in Figure 3-5. The bidirectional replication of data keeps the state of all the applications synchronized between both CSPs to allow for failover from either CSP to happen.

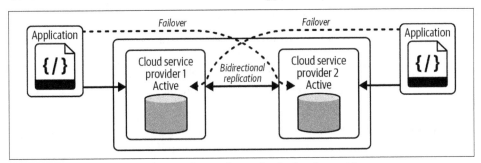

Figure 3-6. An active-active DR solution for multiple cloud providers

In the context of the data mesh, both active-active and active-passive solutions have databases containing the same data (accounting for latency with replication). In the active-passive scenario, capturing data to expose as data products from the passive database would allow you to limit access to the active database. In the active-active scenario, capturing data from one of either active operational database would be acceptable. Both scenarios have their own advantages in a streaming data mesh, depending on the resiliency guarantees offered by the producing domains.

Analytics

Many applications that aren't as resilient don't need cross-CSP disaster recovery, yet may still use services they prefer on other CSPs. For example, the operational plane's data stores may reside in one CSP, and the analytical plane may reside in another CSP. This is a common practice since many data science teams prefer to use specific tools that may exist in only one CSP. In such cases, it is clear to treat the operational and analytical planes as different domains that share data through the data mesh.

Avoiding Ambiguous Domains

Without clearly defined boundaries, domains appear to be too interconnected, and ownership becomes either political or subject to interpretation. For instance, a large retailer most likely has multiple domains. One might be a set of product attributes as they relate to product SKU. Another set of data may relate to its customers, containing attributes that define their demographic profile. These two domains live independently and can be maintained by the respective teams that understand the appropriate business context. These domains can be transformed and published into data products that can be consumed by yet another domain, such as the transactional sales data domain. The transactional sales data domain can then provide data products that not only publish sales data, but also merge in interesting product attributes and customer information that can drive reporting and data science.

To overcome ambiguous domain challenges, each domain boundary must be distinct and explicit. Business area, processes, and data that belong together need to stay together. Additionally, each data domain should belong to one, and only one, Agile or DevOps team. Data integration points within a data domain should be manageable and understood by all team members.

We recommend making domain boundaries concrete and immutable. This helps avoid lengthy discussions about who owns what data, and also prohibits teams from freely interpreting domain boundaries to suit their own needs. Creating a domain-oriented structure is a transition—not only for data, but for people and resources. When creating domain boundaries, resources may eventually align with other teams, disrupting and evolving the current team structure. The entire concept of data mesh is just as much about resource alignment as it is about data, so the realignment of resources should not be considered a roadblock as you go through this process.

As we mentioned earlier, complications arise from data that is shared across domains. In many cases, a shared data domain is suggested, which provides integration logic in a way that allows other domains to standardize and benefit from it. It is important to keep this shared domain small and its naming conventions generalized to fit within the logical context of other domains.

For overlapping data requirements, domain-driven design provides patterns to deal with this complexity. Table 3-1 is a short summary of these patterns.[1]

Table 3-1. Domain-driven design patterns

Pattern	Application
Separate Ways pattern	This can be used if the associated cost of duplication is preferred over reusability. This pattern is typically chosen when reusability is preferred over higher flexibility and agility.
Customer-Supplier pattern	This pattern can be applied if one particular domain is strong and willing to take ownership of data and needs of downstream consumers. The downside of this approach can be conflicting priorities, forcing downstream teams to negotiate deliverables and prioritize story points.
Partnership pattern	In this approach, integration logic is coordinated on an as-needed basis within a newly created domain. All teams cooperate and coordinate with regard to one another's needs. Orchestration and consensus is required from all team members because each team is not allowed to change the shared model at will.
Conformist pattern	This approach can be used to conform all domains to all requirements. This pattern can be a choice when (1) the integration work is extremely complex, (2) no parties are allowed to have control, or (3) vendor packages are used.

Domain-Driven Design

For the source-aligned domain data and application team techniques of identifying domains, if your applications and related sources aren't yet defined, you need a methodology to help define them. *Domain-driven design* (DDD) is the methodology that helps us understand complex domain models by connecting the data model itself to core business concepts. The understanding that emerges from DDD creates a foundation to designing distributed, microservice-based, client-facing applications.

DDD connects the implementation of software and its components to an evolving and ever-changing data model. The domain is the world of the business you are working with and the problems you are trying to solve. This typically involves rules, processes, and existing systems that need to be integrated as part of your solution.

DDD was first introduced by Eric Evans in *Domain-Driven Design* (Addison-Wesley Professional). The book focuses on three principles:

- The primary focus is the core *domain* and *domain logic*.
- Complex designs are based on *models of the domain*.
- Collaboration between technical and *domain experts* is crucial to creating an application model that will solve defined domain problems.

---

1 Piethein Strengholt, *Data Management at Scale* (O'Reilly).

When doing DDD, it is important to understand the following terms:

- Domain model
- Domain logic
- Bounded context
- Ubiquitous language

Domain Model

The *domain model* encompasses all ideas, knowledge, metrics, and goals that relate to the problem you are trying to solve. The domain model represents the vocabulary and key concepts of the problem domain and should identify the relationships among all the entities within the scope of the domain. Many software projects suffer from a lack of common terminology, objectives, and proposed solutions that are scoped at the beginning of development. This is where the domain model fits in—it acts as a clear depiction of the problem being solved and the proposed solution. Moreover, the domain is the world of your business, the model becomes the solution, and the domain model acts as structured knowledge about the problem.

> The terms *objects*, *models*, and *entities* are used interchangeably in this book. They may be used with the terms *business model, business object, domain model, business entity,* or *domain entity*. They all mean the same thing.

Domain Logic

The *domain logic* represents the reasons or purposes the domain exists. Other terms that could be used are *business logic, business rules,* or *domain knowledge*. Domain logic is defined in the domain entities, which are a combination of data and behavior. They enforce the logic in and between the entities that ultimately provides a solution to a problem the domain is tasked to solve.

Bounded Context

Bounded contexts are boundaries in DDD where logic and complexity cluster together. They help organize business logic and entities into groups to increase modularity and agility, which could create domains and subdomains. These ultimately can become data mesh domains or subdomains.

The Ubiquitous Language

The *ubiquitous language* builds a vernacular so domain experts and developers can simplify communication while designing a domain. Gaps can form between personas of a domain if a ubiquitous language is not built—for example, articulating concerns in the domain model so that an engineer can propagate a technical issue to the business logic level. Conversely, a domain expert being able to articulate a business logic issue down to lower-level technical exceptions is equally important. This enables all personas to understand the entire spectrum of issues and how to handle and inform users of their solution.

The outcome of DDD is a solution to building an application that follows an EDA. Engineers design applications using the EDA pattern, which is a based on events, relationships, business rules, bounded contexts, and the ubiquitous language defined during the DDD process. The events and entities that are generated in the application become data in the business domain and potentially can become data products in the streaming data mesh.

Following DDD, domain experts help define business objects and ensure they fit in the greater context of the business. For example, *account* and *employee* could be considered business objects within a domain. These business objects get turned into data products in the data mesh. This may require meeting with other domain teams that may claim the same or similar business objects that another domain is planning to serve. As previously discussed in this chapter, it may make sense to create a shared data domain or create replicas of shared data, depending on business requirements.

Data Mesh Domain Roles

A domain has two main roles: data product engineer (or just data engineer) and the data product owner (or data product manager, or data steward). These roles can be the same or dedicated people in the domain.

Data product owners must have a deep understanding of who their data consumers are, how the data is used, and what methods are used to consume the data. This will help ensure that the data products meet the needs of their use cases. Data product engineers are responsible for creating data products that are high quality, reliable, and usable by consumers. It should be possible to extend existing domain roles to include these domain roles with minimal effort.

Data Product Engineer

Probably the most important role within a data mesh domain, the *data product engineer*, is responsible for building, maintaining, and serving a data domain's data products. This includes the tasks associated with ingesting data from operational databases, transforming these data assets, and publishing them to the data mesh. See Table 3-2 for the list of tasks for the data product engineer.

Table 3-2. Data product engineer tasks

Task	Details
Data ingestion	• Deploy an integration solution to get data from its source into the streaming platform.
Transformation	• Cleanse data by ensuring the attributes all conform to the data types defined by the data product model or follow a standardized format. • Enrich the data using SQL joins or aggregations.
Data governance	• Ensure data is tokenized or encrypted in accordance to data privacy regulations. • Preserve lineage or "recursive lineage" if consuming data products from other domains. • Maintain transitive data governance when publishing data products derived from data products from other domains.
Scaling	• Allow more consumers of the data products.

Data Product Owner or Data Steward

A *data product owner*, or *data steward*, role is semi-technical, intended to primarily understand data usage patterns and ensure that consumers are satisfied with each data product. We will use the term data product owner. This person communicates with both end users and data product engineers, and works to improve and evolve the product. See Table 3-3 for a list of tasks related to the data product owner.

Table 3-3. Data product owner/data steward tasks

Tasks	Details
Security	• Grant access to data products. • Ensure that security meets InfoSec requirements. This includes authorization, authentication, and data governance.
Observability	• Monitor data products for throughput performance, quality, and user satisfaction. • Monitor usage metrics and provide that information to the data catalog and centralized observability tool.
Data governance	• Participate in the decision making in federated data governance to establish best practices and maintain interoperability that promotes overall data mesh health. • May also participate in the decision making in federated data governance.
Maintaining data product lifecycle	• Promote to production and publish to the data mesh. • Manage versioning of data products. • Manage data product bugs. • Organize feature requests for data products. • Manage data product evolution: versioning, EOL.
Performance	• Receive feedback from data product owner on performance and user satisfaction. • Define the scale of the data product pipeline as well as its serving layer. • Find solutions to improve SLAs and user satisfaction from an architectural perspective.

Tasks	Details
Costs	• Monitoring the cost related to infrastructure and usage. • Calculate the charge-back costs to the consumers.

The data product owner also ensures that infrastructure is provisioned (using self-service tools) and in place with the proper resources to develop and deliver data products to the data mesh and ensure that data is highly available, meets SLAs, and implements all necessary security measures. This role continually monitors usage and cost, ensuring that customers are satisfied, while minimizing any incurred charges.

Streaming Data Mesh Tools and Platforms to Consider

To implement a streaming data mesh, we will look to existing tools and platforms. Table 3-4 shows some of the most useful and popular tools and platforms.

Table 3-4. High-level tools to use

Platform and tools	Example
Streaming data platform	Apache Kafka, Redpanda, Apache Pulsar
Integration solution to move data from operational data store to streaming platform	Kafka Connect
Stream processing tool, allowing data product engineers to transform and clean data products	ksqlDB, Apache Flink, SaaS stream processor
Tool to edit and publish schemas that define domain objects	Schema Registry
Data catalog	Apache Atlas, Amundsen

The chosen tools and platforms determine how the ports of a domain will be implemented—in other words, how the domains will produce and consume streaming data products from one another.

Domain Charge-Backs

In an enterprise, each line of business has a budget to keep operations humming along. In a standard data warehousing environment, the party responsible party for paying for required data services is relatively clear. However, when data ownership is decentralized and distributed, such as in a data mesh, who pays for all this content becomes unclear. As costs for standing up data domains and data products increase, it is important to distribute these costs to consumers of the data mesh. The following are some examples of how to divide incurred cost of deploying a data mesh at the domain level:

Usage-based charge-backs

One solution for domain charge-back is to associate specific container instances with downstream users or teams. This solution works well when you want to restrict hosting of services for downstream consumers at an instance level. This method, however, has drawbacks. First, as a cluster of instances is initially provisioned for end users, it is easy to over-provision and cause the consumer to pay for more resources than they actually need. Secondly, as services are shared across a data domain, it may become apparent that resources are being consumed that weren't initially charged for. As a result, it may be necessary to place resource constraints on certain data products, potentially impacting SLAs.

Task-level resource charge-backs

Another solution could be to develop a mechanism to let the data domain owners calculate the aggregate cost of each data product. This solution requires developing a metering mechanism and charge-back measurement. As the metering mechanism is deployed, it tracks request usage, including network, vCPU, and memory to service such requests. Then, with charge-back measurement in place, domain owners can easily associate a cost with these tasks based on the cost incurred by container instances that the domain is running on. This solution allows domain owners to deploy their entire solution on shared infrastructure without the intricacies of usage-based charge-back and its limitations. Costs of domain usage can be calculated at any point in time, for any cluster, and any data product.

Cost-splitting charge-backs

There may be certain well-known consumers of data products within a domain. In this case, rather than calculating the cost of domain usage on a per-request basis or on a usage-based pattern, it may make sense for groups to agree to split the cost of data product consumption at the domain level. Groups would agree to split the overall calculated cost of domain operation across multiple consumers, each one being responsible for a fixed percentage. The advantage to this approach is ease of deployment, since it does not require a mechanism to monitor usage. The downsides include unpredictable and unexpected usage spikes; consumers using an incorrectly calculated percentage of total resources, thus causing over- or under-billing; and the inability to track actual usage patterns by consumer.

Data products charge-backs

To implement charge-backs, a monitoring tool needs to be provisioned to help measure the usage of the data products and/or the resources used. This monitoring tool can be part of the data mesh control plane and automatically comes with the provisioning of the tools described in Table 3-4. In Chapter 4, we talk about how we can monitor data products to charge-back consumers.

Summary

When defining domains, architects need to consider more than just the business objects defined in a domain-driven design. In this chapter we provided other strategies that need to be considered that would affect domains such as geographic regions, hybrid clouds, multiclouds, and disaster recovery requirements. In Chapter 4, we will show how these domains build and publish streaming data products into the streaming data mesh.

Streaming Data Products

In a streaming data mesh, domains own their data. This creates a decentralized data platform to help resolve the issues relating to agility and scalability in the data lake and warehouses. Domains now have to serve other domains their data. So it's important that they treat their data as products with high quality and trust.

Currently, data engineers are very used to the idea that all their data is in a central data store like a data lake or warehouse. They are used to finding ways to "boil the ocean" (in this case, lake) when working with data. A streaming data mesh allows us to evaporate that idea. In this chapter, we will outline the requirements for streaming data products.

In our careers as data engineers, we have found ourselves writing many wrappers for Apache Spark, a widely used analytics engine for large-scale data processing. Only in the past few years did we fully understand why companies asked us to do this.

Big data tools like Apache Spark, Apache Flink, and Apache Kafka Streams were inaccessible to many engineers who were tasked to solve big data problems. Referring back to Chapter 1, breaking up the monolithic role of a data engineer is a side effect of a data mesh.

This is a very important point because a second side effect is making complex data engineering tools like Spark, Flink, and Kafka Streams more accessible to generalist engineers so they can solve their big data problems. It's the reason these companies asked us to wrap large-scale data processing engines. Table 4-1 shows a list of projects we were involved with to help specific engineers query big data stored in data lakes.

Table 4-1. Apache Spark wrapper projects and the engineers each project supports

The project	The engineer
Big Data Integrator—an Apache Spark UI wrapper with drag-and-drop features	Integration engineers and business analysts needing to process data to deliver reports in a business intelligence tool.
Sparknado—an Apache Spark wrapper that used Airflow syntax to build Spark DAGs	Airflow engineers build Spark applications to move data into Snowflake.
Apache Envelope—a YAML-based Spark configuration	Engineers who want to define a Spark DAG without needing to know how to code in Python or Scala.
Splunk SPL to Spark—a pipe syntax that resembles Splunk Search Language (SPL)	Security threat hunters who are familiar with Splunk to be able to hunt for threats in network logs stored in a data lake.

Having done this so many times validates the necessity to simplify data tools to be more accessible to generalist and sometimes specialist engineers, and not so much to reduce workload for data engineers. It enables them to react faster to anomalous issues and provide immediate results to customers.

When building data products, it is important to understand this. Enabling domains with access to data tools will enable them to solve complex data problems. This ability was previously out of reach for them.

In the following sections, we will go through the requirements of defining and building data products to be published in a streaming data mesh. We will try to keep the scope of the details to building streaming data products, and we will refer to details regarding self-services and data governance as they relate to streaming data products in their corresponding chapters.

Defining Data Product Requirements

This section is a summary of the requirements for data products listed in Table 4-2. The goal of these requirements is to give consumers and domain consumers a smooth and pleasant data mesh experience. The health of the data mesh is determined by the domain consumer's experience with data products. These requirements will help design and implement a data product that meets the needs of its consumers.

Table 4-2. Suggestions for data product requirements

Requirements	Implementation considerations
Data products should be of high quality.	• The data should be transformed to the standards defined by all the domains in the data mesh. • Bad records should be filtered out as required.
Data products must be secure and trustworthy.	• All personal identifiable information (PII) or personal health information (PHI) should be obfuscated by either tokenization or encryption. • Authorization and authentication is defined as ACLs or RBACs rules.

Requirements	Implementation considerations
Data products must be interoperable.	• Data products should provide schemas that represent the final data product. Schemas serve as a contract between the producing domain and the consuming domain. • Data products should be in a format that supports consumers written in multiple programming languages (polyglot). Some examples are JSON, Apache Avro, and protobuf.
Data products must be easily consumable.	• The data product must be quickly and easily accessible through simple technical means. • The data product must be optimized for reading and serving. Some ways to optimize data are partitioning, indexing, bucketing, and compaction.
Data products should preserve lineage.	• The data lineage must be derived from the metadata recursively through the other domains. For example, if the data product uses another domain's data product, the lineage from the derivative data product is preserved and can be parsed.
Data products should be easily searchable and self-describing.	• The data product should be discoverable using a search engine and is descriptive enough for consumers to have trust in it.
Data products should provide historical data.	• The data product should support serving historical data, not just the latest changes.

Retroactively adding data product requirements could prove to be costly in technical debt. For example, lineage is most likely a requirement that would be hard to retroactively add without the referable metadata needed to build it, so it is important to think of these complex requirements early to avoid costly technical debt.

When other domains request data products, ensure that they adhere to these requirements. Keep them in mind when you identify the sources you'll need to compose your data products.

 Some have confused data products as being mastered data. *Data mastering* is a process of building an undisputed master version of a record called a *golden record*. Master data is a feature of a data product and not necessarily a data product requirement. If your data product is required to provide mastered employee records, for example, then a proper master data management (MDM) tool will be required within the domain to perform this work.

Identifying Data Product Derivatives

Data products are derived from the data sources within a domain. They could also be enriched from data products from other domains. Remember that data products are owned by the domain experts that produced them. If the data product you are building requires enrichment from data from another domain, you'll need to ingest that data into your own domain to enrich your own data products. We are defining *data derivatives* as both data within the domain and data sourced from other domains. Identifying these derivatives and understanding their integration points will help in defining solutions to begin ingesting them into the streaming platform.

There are two types of data: at rest and in motion. We need to start ingesting data derivatives that will involve getting the data at rest to be data in motion. We also want to keep the data already in motion to stay in motion. It is important to think of optimization of data early in the ingestion process so that any downstream components can take advantage of this optimization. Start with partitioning the data in the source topics in the streaming platform. Having enough partitions will efficiently serve data products to consumers and create balanced processing in the data pipeline.

Derivatives from Other Domains

Derivatives that originate from other domains as data products need to be referable so that a full lineage picture can be generated. This could include multiple domains traversed recursively throughout the mesh. Preserving a snapshot of the current lineage of a data product will eventually get stale as the data product derivatives may have evolved in quality, scalability, and structure, as in schemas. In later chapters, we will discuss data governance and schema evolution as a centralized component in the data mesh. Techniques for preserving lineage will be discussed more in Chapter 6.

Consuming other data products from other domains and enriching your own is the true essence of working in a data mesh. The experience will involve requesting access to the data product and then subscribing to the real-time stream of the data product. After this is done, a topic in the streaming platform should appear that represents the real-time streaming data product originating from another domain. Part of this data product subscription is not only to the data but also to the metadata. It is this metadata that will enable lineage that spans multiple domains.

Ingesting Data Product Derivatives with Kafka Connect

After identifying the data product derivatives for our streaming data products, we need to get them into a streaming platform. The simplest way to get data into or out of a Kafka-compliant streaming platform is to leverage Kafka connectors. (Other platforms such as Spark or Flink also have their own connectors.) *Kafka Connect* is a framework that enables implementation for reading data from a data source and into a streaming platform. Conversely, it also enables implementation for writing data to a data sink from the streaming platform. See Figure 4-1.

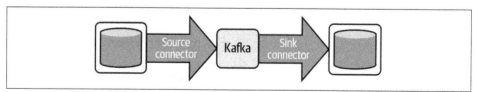

Figure 4-1. A data pipeline that illustrates a Kafka source connector writing to Kafka, and a Kafka sink connector reading from Kafka

Kafka Connect also provides low-code experience, which means that no coding is required for domain engineers. We will use Kafka Connect as our way of ingesting source data into the streaming platform. There are other ways of ingesting data into a streaming platform, but not many support the change data capture (CDC) connectors that we need. We will talk about CDC in "Debezium Connectors" on page 54.

The Kafka Connect open source framework allows for simple ingress and egress of data in a scalable way. It's one of the reasons we've chosen this solution to discuss. Connectors are able to connect to specific data sources as well as a Kafka-compliant streaming platform to stream data, such as Redpanda. Other products, such as Apache Pulsar, allow Kafka clients to produce and consume messages from Kafka into their platform.

Kafka connectors do not run by themselves. They run in a Kafka Connect cluster that enables them to be distributable and highly available. Each node in the connect cluster is called a *connect worker*. Every connector contains a configuration property called `tasks.max`. *Tasks* are the main processes that stream data in a connector. When configured with multiple tasks, the connect cluster is able to distribute them across its workers to run in parallel, enabling scalability. If one of the connect workers in the cluster were to suffer an outage, the data is redistributed across the remaining workers (see Figure 4-2). The `task.max` property defines the maximum number of tasks that should be created for this connector in a connect cluster. The connector may create fewer tasks if it cannot achieve this level of parallelism.

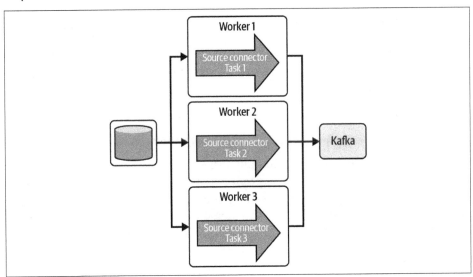

Figure 4-2. A single source connector whose three tasks are distributed across three connect workers in a Kafka Connect cluster; connect workers can be deployed into separate machines for high availability and scalability

Using Kafka Connect and the many prebuilt connectors makes building the streaming data mesh a lot faster and relinquishes the development and support to third-party vendors. Connectors for popular databases and cloud data stores have already been built. Many of them are developed by the vendors themselves and come with support plans. If a connector is not available, the centralized data mesh team should have the skill set to build one and provide it to the domains in the data mesh for use.

Another reason Kafka Connect is a good solution is that it standardizes ingestion, simplifying connector deployment and management. The Kafka Connect cluster provides a RESTful interface and can integrate easily with a CI/CD pipeline like Jenkins, Kubernetes, Ansible, or Terraform.

Kafka Connect has some transformation capabilities called *single message transforms* (SMTs), but these are limited to simple transformations. That means no joins or aggregations. Data transformation is best consolidated in the streaming processes where both simple and complex transformations are supported. Transformations will be covered in "Transforming Data Derivatives to Data Products" on page 55.

 It is best practice to perform transformations in a stream processor that can hold state and not in the connectors that cannot hold state. Also, capturing transformations in a connector to preserve lineage could be difficult, while stream processors that build directed acyclic graphs (DAGs) representing the processing workflow can serialize their DAGs for lineage preservation.

When ingesting the data product derivatives, we need to think early about the eventual streaming data product and how to ensure its ease of consumption. Also keep in mind that whether the data will be ingested asynchronously or synchronously is a factor that will impact how the domain will consume and use your streaming data product.

Consumability

Consumability is a very important requirement because it will directly affect the experience domain consumers will have in a streaming data mesh. If other domains cannot easily consume streaming data products, then they may opt out of the streaming data mesh and decide to build their own integrations by hand, bypassing any issues they encounter with the data mesh. Some factors to consider when ingesting data derivatives that will affect the consumability of other domains are as follows:

- Lack of scalability
- Lack of interoperability

Scalability

When thinking about ingesting data derivatives into the streaming platform, it is important to know the scale in which you will need to ingest the data. In the streaming platform, you will need to make sure that the number of partitions can support the throughput (or the rate) the data is expected to be streamed. The more partitions in a Kafka topic, the faster it can stream the data. Partitions are how Kafka enables parallelism. In other streaming platforms, you will need to configure their topic equivalents similarly.

A rough formula proposed by Jun Rao (an original developer of Apache Kafka) for determining partition count is based on throughput. This formula gets partition count by finding the max between these two values:

- The desired throughput (t) divided by the throughput of producing data to the partition you can achieve (p)
- The desired throughput (t) divided by the throughput consuming data from the partition you can achieve (c)

The formula is as follows:

$$max(t/p, t/c)$$

The following example shows 3 MBps (megabytes per second) desired throughput. The producer can produce 1 MBps. Let's assume 3 consumers want to subscribe to the data, which means 3 MBps at 1 MBps each. The result is 3 partitions. In this example, the count is actually low for most Kafka use cases. You may want to prepare for future increases in throughput by increasing this count to 5 or 6:

$$max(3 \text{ MBps}/1 \text{ MBps}, 3 \text{ MBps}/3 \text{ MBps}) = max(3, 1) = 3 \text{ partitions}$$

Other factors can help with getting the throughput desired but are beyond the scope of this book.

After determining the number of partitions, understanding how to distribute the data evenly throughout all the partitions is important to achieve balanced parallelism. In Apache Kafka, data is sent as a key and value pair. The key is hashed to determine which partition it will be assigned to. This formula illustrates how this works:

$$key \% p = partition \text{ assignment}$$

This hashing algorithm works well when the key is evenly distributed across all records in the data sent to the Kafka topic. In other words, the key should have high cardinality and even distribution in the entire data set. High cardinality and even distribution creates good data balance among all the topic partitions. Low cardinality or an uneven distribution creates imbalanced parallelism. Imbalanced parallelism at ingestion creates imbalance for all downstream components in the data pipeline. In the Kafka topics, this manifests as hot spotting, where only one or a few partitions are doing most of the work, causing your entire data pipeline to run slowly. It would be beneficial to profile your data to get a sense of your cardinality and distribution of the keys in the data. Defining keys with high cardinality and even distribution is an important step in distributed processing because most distributed systems distribute workload to its workers by key.

Another way of improving scalability is by using a proper data serialization format, which we'll discuss next.

Interoperability and data serialization

Keeping scalability and interoperability in mind is critical as we start to talk about how to actually ingest the data into a streaming platform. *Interoperability* is the ability to exchange information or work seamlessly with other systems. In the case of a streaming data mesh, this can be accomplished by creating schemas that define the domain objects or models and choosing a proper data serialization format. The schemas will help domains in the streaming data mesh easily exchange information and work seamlessly with other domains, and the data serialization format will allow information exchange between systems that normally are incompatible with each other.

Interoperability and data serialization are data mesh requirements that fall under the data governance pillar, discussed in Chapter 5, so we'll go into more detail there. But it's critical that we start thinking about them at data ingestion because this affects all the systems and data pipeline components downstream. First, we need to define the schema that represents the data derivative. A *schema* is basically a definition of how the data will be structured when it moves through the streaming data pipeline. For example, let's say you're ingesting COVID-19 global statistics. The shape of your data may look like Table 4-3, which provides only two countries. (Note that Table 4-4 is a continuation of the data in Table 4-3.)

Table 4-3. COVID-19 mock data in a table format

Country	CountryCode	Date	ID
United States of America	USA	2022-04-07T19:47:08.275Z	2291245c-5bf8-460f-af77-05ce78cc60c9
Philippines	PH	2022-04-07T19:47:08.275Z	82aa04f7-05a1-4caa-b309-0e7cfbfae5ea

Table 4-4. COVID-19 mock data in a table format (continued)

NewConfirmed	NewDeaths	NewRecovered	TotalConfirmed	TotalDeaths	TotalRecovered
40176	1241	0	80248986	983817	0
0	0	0	3680244	59422	0

The COVID-19 data source we are reading is served as JSON records, so we would create the data serialization format as JSON. In Example 4-1 we show a JSON schema definition that matches the structure of Table 4-3.

Example 4-1. JSON schema that defines the table structure in Table 4-3

```
{
  "$schema": "http://json-schema.org/draft-04/schema#",
  "type": "object",
  "properties": {  ❶
    "ID": {
      "type": "string"
    },
    "Country": {
      "type": "string"
    },
    "CountryCode": {
      "type": "string"
    },
    "NewConfirmed": {
      "type": "integer"
    },
    "TotalConfirmed": {
      "type": "integer"
    },
    "NewDeaths": {
      "type": "integer"
    },
    "TotalDeaths": {
      "type": "integer"
    },
    "NewRecovered": {
      "type": "integer"
    },
    "TotalRecovered": {
      "type": "integer"
    },
    "Date": {
      "type": "string"
    }
  },
  "required": [  ❷
    "ID",
    "Country",
    "CountryCode",
    "NewConfirmed",
    "TotalConfirmed",
    "NewDeaths",
    "TotalDeaths",
    "NewRecovered",
    "TotalRecovered",
```

```
    "Date"
  ]
}
```

❶ Lists the fields and their data types

❷ Lists the fields that are required

Table 4-5 shows some data serialization formats to choose from that are suited for streaming data. Many other serialization formats exist, like Parquet and ORC, but those aren't suited for streaming data. They are more suited for data at rest in data lakes.

Table 4-5. Data serialization formats supported in streaming

Name	Maintainer	Binary	Human readable
JSON	Douglas Crockford	No	Yes
Apache Avro	Apache Software Foundation	Yes	Partial
Protocol Buffers (protobuf)	Google	Yes	Partial

Many data serialization formats, like Parquet and ORC, help queries run more efficiently in a data lake. Others improve performance in a service mesh (microservice intercommunication) like Avro and protobuf. JSON is probably the most used data serialization format because of its easy use and human readability.

All the options in Table 4-5 can be defined by a schema. We will talk more about how these schemas create contracts between producing and consuming domains and their roles in supporting data governance in the streaming data mesh in Chapter 5.

Synchronous Data Sources

At the beginning of this section we spoke about how domains will consume streaming data products—synchronously or asynchronously. Let's first describe synchronous data consumption in terms of client and server, where the client is requesting data and the server serves the data.

Synchronous (also referred to as *batch*) data consumption means the consumer (the client) of the data follows a request-and-response relationship with the server. The client requests data from a data service, and the service quickly returns a snapshot of the result from the source.

When requesting these pages, you are requesting results using frameworks like ODBC or JDBC to connect and retrieve these batches from a data source. This approach forces you to capture snapshots of data that follow batching semantics. Each snapshot is considered a batch.

Figure 4-3 shows the client requesting the initial snapshot of the data from the database. When the client requests another snapshot, you have to subtract the second from the initial snapshot to find only the incremental changes. Or, you can overwrite the initial snapshot with the second snapshot, but you'll lose what changed. If database changes need to trigger an action, you will need to find the incremental changes.

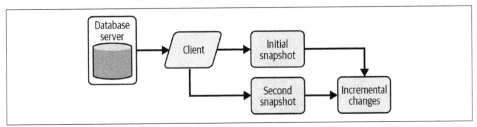

Figure 4-3. Determining incremental changes from a database snapshot

Additionally, if changes occur between client snapshots, you will miss changes that revert to its original value. In Table 4-6, the events that changed from Robert to Bob and then back to Robert again are lost.

Table 4-6. Changes lost between snapshots

Time	Events
12:00	Initial snapshot
12:01	Name changed from Robert to Bob
12:03	Name changed back from Bob to Robert
12:05	Second snapshot

This example illustrates how synchronous data APIs force clients requesting data into batching semantics that could lead to some data loss, as seen with incremental snapshots. Some event-driven application systems will try to use synchronous APIs and adapt them to real-time data streams. We see this quite often because many systems don't have support for streaming, so we are left to emulate a data stream emitting from those data sources.

Consumers of this data will need to know that the results are taken using snapshots and to expect to lose some data.

Asynchronous Data Sources and Change Data Capture

Asynchronous data sources follow a different approach: clients subscribe to changes to data instead of taking snapshots. Anytime a change is made, an entry is made in the change log, and the clients subscribed to it get notified and can react to the change. This is called *change data capture* (CDC).

Kafka connectors that support CDC read the database commit log and capture the changes to a database table. These changes are real-time streams of database table changes, including inserts, updates, and deletes. This means you don't lose the changes described in Table 4-6.

 If possible, ingest data derivatives by CDC and not by snapshots to ensure that all transactions are captured.

Referring back to "Data Divide" on page 3, the goal was to move data from the operational databases to the analytical plane. Those operational databases hold transactions that power the business. Losing transactions between snapshots could be a critical problem in many use cases. It is best to utilize a Kafka connector that can perform CDC from the operational database and stream it to the streaming platform.

Debezium Connectors

A set of CDC connectors called Debezium connectors (*https://oreil.ly/k0k1m*) capture changes in a database from a change log and send them to a streaming platform. The most commonly used connectors are as follows:

- MySQL CDC
- MongoDB
- PostgreSQL
- Oracle
- SQL Server
- IBM Db2
- Apache Cassandra
- Vitess

For non-Kafka streaming platforms, a Debezium server can be used as an alternative to running a Kafka Connect cluster. Figure 4-4 illustrates how the Debezium server can replace the Kafka Connect cluster to send to other streaming platforms. Change events can be serialized to different formats like JSON or Apache Avro, and then sent to one of a variety of messaging systems.

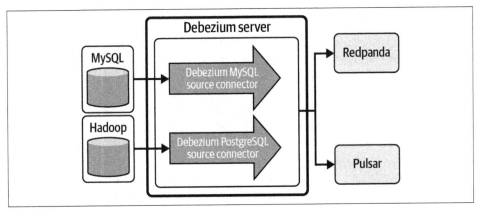

Figure 4-4. A Debezium server replacing a Kafka Connect cluster to serve connectors to alternative streaming platforms: Redpanda and Apache Pulsar

The Debezium server can also serve other streaming platforms that do not have a commit log. Those platforms do not appear in Figure 4-4. It is important to remember that only streaming platforms that hold data in a commit log can best support Kappa architectures and ultimately a streaming data mesh, as mentioned in Chapter 2.

Thinking about consumability early will save you from complaints from domain consumers later. Making clear how the streaming data products are retrieved (synchronous or asynchronous) will help them understand what to expect.

The result of ingesting data into a streaming platform will be a topic for each data derivative. We will transform and enrich these derivatives to compose the final streaming data product.

Transforming Data Derivatives to Data Products

In the previous section, we ingested the data derivatives so that our streaming data products would be consumable, focusing on scalability and interoperability. This section will focus on transforming data derivatives to ensure that our streaming data products are of high quality and secure.

We will also suggest some easy tools for transforming data derivatives into streaming data products. These tools will leverage SQL to transform data. Using SQL is a skill set ubiquitous to many engineers, including domain engineers. It is the preferred way of enabling domain engineers to build streaming data products.

Data Standardization

It is a best practice to establish format standards when sharing data with other domains. These standards are part of a set of data governance polices enforced for all domains (we will cover data governance in Chapter 5). Standardizing data creates consistency across your domains and makes the data easy for them to use. Otherwise, all domains will need to know how to convert different formats for every domain that doesn't follow the standard. So as part of transforming data derivatives, we will need to transform data to adhere to these standards. For example, data governance policies may require all phone numbers to be in a standard format like 1-234-567-8900. But the original source data may not provide the numbers in that format. We need to make sure all the formatting standards are applied to the data before it is published as a streaming data product.

Protecting Sensitive Information

You must also ensure that sensitive information is obfuscated by tokenizing, encrypting, or omitting it. For example, protected health information (PHI) and personally identifiable information (PII) are considered sensitive data. PHI and PII data is subject to regulatory rules like the Health Insurance Portability and Accountability Act (HIPAA) and the General Data Protection Regulation (GDPR). Regulations beyond HIPAA and GDPR are beyond the scope of this book.

The HIPAA privacy rule protects all individually identifiable health information held or transmitted by a covered entity or its business associate, in any form or media, whether electronic, paper, or oral. The privacy rule calls this information "protected health information (PHI)." Individually identifiable health information is information, including demographic data, that relates to any of the following:[1]

- The individual's past, present, or future physical or mental health or condition
- The provision of health care to the individual
- The past, present, or future payment for the provision of health care to the individual

GDPR requires companies across the EU to protect the privacy of, and safeguard the data they keep on, their employees, customers, and third-party vendors. Companies are now under legal obligation to keep this PII safe and secure.[2]

---

[1] US Department of Health and Human Services, "Summary of the HIPAA Privacy Rule" (*https://oreil.ly/1w33M*), p. 4.

[2] The EU's GDPR (*https://gdpr.eu*) applies only to personal data, which is any piece of information that relates to an identifiable person. It's crucial for any business with EU consumers to understand this concept for GDPR compliance.

Table 4-7 shows a few methods for obfuscating sensitive data such as PHI and PII to keep within the regulations that protect them.

Table 4-7. Examples of obfuscating sensitive data

Method	Purpose
Tokenization	Replaces the data with a token. Later, the token can be looked up to get the original value as long as the system looking up the token has permission to retrieve it. Often, tokenizing data maintains its original format and exposes a partial value. For example, a credit card number may show the last four digits: xxxx-xxxx-xxxx-1234
Encryption	Replaces the value with an encrypted value. The value can be decrypted with a key. A system can request to decrypt the data to get its original value as long as it has the key. The format is not preserved in this method. Here is a credit card example: 1234-5678-9012-3456 encrypted to MTIzNDEyMzQxMjM0MTIzNAo=
Filtering	This method omits the sensitive information entirely.

The SQL language can be extended with user-defined functions to allow for these obfuscation methods, which we will talk more about in the next section.

SQL

As mentioned before, SQL is the language of choice for streaming data product transformations because it's accessible to many domain engineers. Therefore, we will have to choose a streaming data processing platform that supports SQL. There are not many streaming data processing engines at the time of this writing. We will go over two options: a SaaS stream processor and ksqlDB.

SaaS stream processor

A *SaaS stream processor* is a cloud SaaS product that uses SQL to transform data consumed from a streaming platform like Kafka. They tend to be implemented on Apache Flink (which offers truly native streaming) as opposed to Apache Spark structured streaming (which offers low-latency microbatches that only emulate streaming). Apache Flink processes events in real time with lower latency compared to Apache Spark structured streaming.

Apache Flink is not seen in the user interfaces. A SQL interface is shown to the user instead. Data product engineers can consume from a streaming platform like Kafka, perform stateful transformations, and then write the output to a sink or another streaming platform, as shown in Figure 4-5.

Flink's model for stream processing includes a component called connectors that acts as data sources and sinks (similar to Kafka connectors). The component called stream represents streaming data that holds streams of data. Lastly, a component called pipeline can join and aggregate streams using SQL to create new streams. Altogether, these components create a simple and easy-to-use data processing tool to build streaming data pipelines.

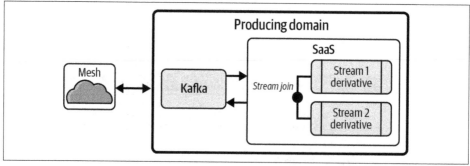

Figure 4-5. SaaS stream processor joining/enriching data derivatives, one of which is a data product from another domain, and publishing back to the mesh

Apache Flink also enables domains to replicate data from the producing domain into their own, ultimately building the mesh, as shown in Figure 4-6.

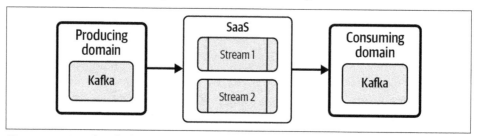

Figure 4-6. Apache Flink replicating data from the producing to the consuming domain

Each `stream` in Flink represents streaming data that can be treated as a new streaming data product and consumed by many other domains.

A great advantage with Flink is that it can consume from many Kafka clusters. It can also consume from alternative streaming platforms, like Redpanda and Apache Pulsar, and join them in a single streaming pipeline. In addition, it can mix streaming platforms (such as RabbitMQ or Kinesis) that do not utilize a commit log, thus providing a fully agnostic stream processing solution, as shown in Figure 4-7.

Apache Flink can also provide self-services to easily provision and author streaming data pipelines. It removes the tasks of provisioning infrastructure and writing code that require specialized skills.

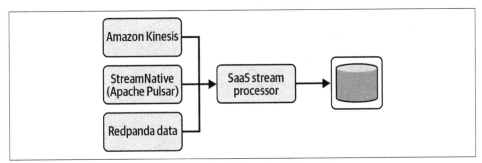

Figure 4-7. A streaming pipeline implemented as SQL that can join multiple streaming platforms, even ones that do not utilize a commit log, to enable event sourcing

ksqlDB

ksqlDB is another stream processing tool that provides a SQL interface for building data pipelines on top of Kafka. ksqlDB's SQL-like language abstracts away the actual implementation of Kafka Streams underneath. ksqlDB creates table-like structures from Kafka topics. It can join and aggregate data between Kafka topics and provide Kappa architecture capabilities.

ksqlDB follows the highly recognized SQL-92 standard, which is the third revision of the standard. This is defined by the American National Standards Institute (ANSI), which is responsible for maintaining this standard for SQL specifications.

A ksqlDB deployment is limited to a single Kafka cluster. It cannot combine multiple streaming platforms. It does provide a way to provision connectors. It allows domain engineers to stay entirely within a single tool to build streaming data pipelines.

Provisioning connectors in ksqlDB. ksqlDB not only executes stateful transformations, but also has the unique ability to create Kafka connectors to ingress and egress data. Domain engineers no longer have to exit a tool to import and export data. From a single ksqlDB command-line interface (CLI), domain engineers can build an entire data pipeline from sources to published data products completely within the Kappa architecture pattern.

Example 4-2 shows how to create a source Kafka connector. In this example, a Debezium CDC source connector will be connecting to a MySQL database. The connector will read all operations in the order in which they are committed to the database: inserts, updates, and deletes.

Example 4-2. ksqlDB statement that creates a Kafka source connector to bring data into Kafka; a stream/table could then be created from the resulting topic

```
/* creates a connector that reads from MySQL */
CREATE SOURCE CONNECTOR app_data WITH ( ❶
    'connector.class': 'io.debezium.connector.mysql.MySqlConnector', ❷
    'tasks.max': '1', ❸
    'database.hostname': 'mysql', ❹
    'database.port': '3306',
    'database.user': 'debezium',
    'database.password': 'dbz',
    'database.server.id': '184054',
    'database.server.name': 'dbserver1',
    'database.include.list': 'inventory',
    'database.history.kafka.bootstrap.servers': 'kafka:9092', ❺
    'database.history.kafka.topic': 'schema-changes.inventory'
);
```

❶ SOURCE keyword for source connectors.

❷ `io.debezium.connector.mysql.MySqlConnector` is the class name of the connector. If building your own connector, its class name will go here.

❸ The number of tasks that the connector will create.

❹ The hostname of the database.

❺ The Kafka bootstrap server.

Similarly, in Example 4-3, you can create a sink connector to take data out of the streaming platform. In this case, the statement creates a sink connector taking data from a Kafka topic and writing it into an Amazon S3 sink.

Example 4-3. ksqlDB statement creating a Kafka sink connector that reads from a topic and writes to a destination

```
/* creates a connector that writes to a data lake */
CREATE SINK CONNECTOR training WITH ( ❶
    'connector.class': 'S3_SINK', ❷
    'tasks.max': '1',
    'aws.access.key.id': '$AWS_ACCESS_KEY_ID', ❸
    'aws.secret.access.key': '$AWS_SECRET_ACCESS_KEY', ❹
    's3.bucket.name': '$S3_BUCKET', ❺
    'time.interval' : 'HOURLY', ❻
    'data.format': 'BYTES',
    'topics': '$KAFKA_TOPIC_NAME_OUT2'
);
```

❶ SINK keyword for sink connectors.

❷ S3_SINK is an alias to the class name of the S3 sink connector.

❸ The AWS access key.

❹ The AWS secret.

❺ The S3 bucket.

❻ Sets how your messages are grouped in the S3 bucket. Valid entries are DAILY or HOURLY.

You can define transformations between the source and sink statements to create a streaming data pipeline. You can also save the SQL statements in a file to be executed at once. This can be used to promote your streaming data pipeline from development, to staging, then finally to production.

User-defined functions in ksqlDB. In ksqlDB, you are limited to the SQL language when defining streaming data transformations. It does not have the ability to represent complex logic that imperative programming languages can, like C++, Java, Python, etc. To perform more complex logic, a user-defined function (UDF) could be written in Java to hold the complex logic that could not be represented in SQL. That UDF could then be called in ksqlDB without breaking the SQL grammar that ksqlDB uses.

Example 4-4 shows an example of a ksqlDB UDF that multiplies two numbers together. The annotations applied to the Java source enable ksqlDB class loaders to register this UDF as an available function to use.

Example 4-4. A ksqlDB user-defined function that is loaded by ksqlDB and can be used as a function in a ksqlDB statement

```
package com.example;

import io.confluent.ksql.function.udf.Udf;
import io.confluent.ksql.function.udf.UdfDescription;
import io.confluent.ksql.function.udf.UdfParameter;

import java.util.Map;

@UdfDescription(name = "Mul", ❶
                author = "example user",
                version = "1.0.2",
                description = "Multiplies 2 numbers together")
public class MulUdf {
```

```
@Udf(description = "Multiplies 2 integers together.") ❷
public long formula(@UdfParameter int v1, @UdfParameter int v2) { ❸
    return (v1 * v2);
}

@Udf(description = "Multiplies 2 doubles together")
public long formula(@UdfParameter double v1, @UdfParameter double v2) {
    return ((int) (Math.ceil(v1) * Math.ceil(v2)));
}
```

```
}
```

❶ @UdfDescription provides a description of the class.

❷ @Udf identifies the UDF.

❸ @UdfParameter identifies the parameters in the function.

This function permits function overloading to allow for multiple data types. Example 4-5 shows how this can be done.

Example 4-5. An example of how to use the UDF in a ksqlDB statement

```
select formula(col1, col2) as product ❶
from mytable
emit changes; ❷
```

❶ Invocation of the formula function.

❷ Specifies a push query with a continuous output. Push queries are unbounded, or in other words, they do not end because results are continuously being pushed to the consumer. Conversely, pull queries are bounded or eventually end.

 Authoring UDFs in Java may not be a skill accessible to domain engineers. In this case, the centralized data mesh team, which has the necessary skills, should code the UDFs. The data engineers who previously developed and maintained the data pipelines in the data lake will now be part of the central data mesh team.

We covered two solutions for transforming data derivatives in this section. Both used SQL to do these transformations. We transform data to ensure that our streaming data products are of high quality and trustable. Another reason for transforming data is to add more information to the data product so that it can be more useful to domain consumers. In the next section we will talk about how to enrich data using data warehousing concepts.

Extract, Transform, and Load

Now, let's talk about transforming data in an *extract, transform, and load (ETL)* process. Traditionally, this process extracts data from a data source, transforms it to a format that can be consumed by its consumers, and then loads it into a system where these consumers can read it (such as a data lake or data warehouse). ETL is a pattern typically used to collate data from multiple disparate systems into a single centralized system like a data warehouse, as shown in Figure 4-8.

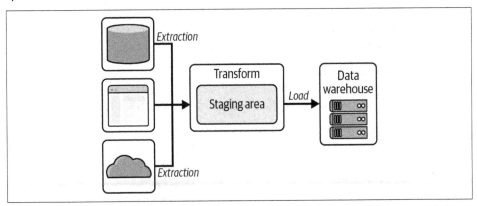

Figure 4-8. An ETL data pipeline that extracts data from multiple sources, writes it into a data lake for staging and transformation, and then loads it into a data warehouse for consumption

The staging area in Figure 4-8 is where transformations are performed. The staging area will typically be a data lake because it can hold a large amount of data. The transformation is executed by massively parallel processing (MPP) applications as well as batch jobs, which then send the data to a data warehouse.

The operational database is the source of information for the data warehouse. It includes detailed information used to run the day-to-day operations of the business. Data frequently changes in the operational database as updates are made to reflect the current value of the last business transactions. To accomplish this, online transaction processing (OLTP) databases are used to manage the changing nature of data in real time.

Data warehouse systems serve as data stores that empower users and decision makers to make business decisions. These systems can organize and present information in specific formats to accommodate the diverse needs of various users. These systems are often referred to as online analytical processing (OLAP) systems.

Operational databases and data warehouses are both relational databases, but each serves different purposes. *Operational database systems* handle both operational and transactional data. *Operational data* consists of data contained in the operations of a particular system or business unit. For example, in retail or e-tail, an operational database handles discrete purchases of items in real time, as well as keeps track of item inventory. A *data warehouse*, on the other hand, holds the historical record of transactions that occur over large amounts of time. For instance, if a large online retailer wants to track the performance of a particular brand or item over the last 10 years, this can be accomplished by querying the data warehouse. This may provide useful information such as performance of ad campaigns, show seasonal trends in buying behavior, or even help to better understand overall brand market share.

The major difference between an operational database and a data warehouse is that, while an operational database is volatile and subject to constant updating, the data warehouse is a historical snapshot of the most current state of any transaction.

Not all data within a data warehouse changes at the same rate. Keeping with the current retail example, a customer's total basket may change many times, and the state of their shopping cart will change with every addition and removal of an item until the customer decides to check out and finalize a purchase. Product characteristics, such as brand, size, color, flavor, or weight, change much more slowly than a set of sales transactions. Information about the customer, such as location, age, interests, along with other demographic and firmographic data, may not change at all or may change only when the customer informs us of such a change or when we receive a feed of matched demographics from a third-party source.

Maintaining data warehouse concepts

Even though a data mesh architecture is intended to decompose and decentralize the analytical plane like the data lake or warehouse, the concepts that make these systems successful should not be lost or compromised. The concept of a star schema (a model that resembles a star by separating fact from dimensional data), the way transformations are defined, and the structure of the data make the data model easy to understand and implement. These same concepts can be used outside the data warehouse to help design streaming ETL data pipelines and provide more usable data products.

As we introduced in Chapter 1, data in an enterprise is divided between operational and analytical planes. Domains that reside in the analytical plane differ greatly from domains that reside in the operational plane. Data that is published as data products, sourced from the operational domain, is typically immutable timestamped snapshots of operational data over time. Historically, changes to data products in the analytical plane evolve more slowly than their operational counterparts. Because of this, a data domain in the analytical plane is responsible for efficiently serving and providing data access to large bodies of data to consumers. Data domains provide a view of data to the outside world—views that are published standards for data access. Behind-the-scenes processes, such as ETL, that are used to create the domain are not exposed to downstream consumers.

Data warehousing basics

In today's business climate, organizations need to have reliable reporting and analysis of large amounts of data. Data needs to be consolidated and integrated for different levels of aggregation for various reporting purposes without impacting the organization's operational systems. The data warehouse makes this possible by creating a repository of an organization's electronically stored data, extracted from the operational systems, and making it available for ad hoc queries and scheduled reporting through ETL processes.

Many approaches to building a data warehouse exist, each with its own set of pros and cons. This book focuses on the star schema approach to data warehousing and its applications to data mesh and streaming data mesh. While we are aware of other data warehouse approaches and their potential application to data mesh, such as Data Vault 2.0, this book does not offer specifics for those approaches.

The *star schema* is the simplest form of a dimensional model used in business intelligence and data warehousing. The star schema consists of one or more fact tables that reference any number of dimension tables. As its name indicates, the star schema's physical model resembles a star shape, with a fact table at its center and dimension tables surrounding it, representing the points of a star.

A *fact table* contains all the primary keys of each dimension, and facts or measures associated with those dimensions. *Dimension tables* provide descriptive information for all measurements recorded in the fact table. As dimensions are informational and change much more slowly than fact tables, dimensions are relatively small compared to the fact table. Commonly used dimensions are people, products, place (or geography), and most importantly, time (see Figure 4-9).

Separating fact and dimensional data is extremely important in order to scale a data warehouse. This separation allows attributes about facts to change over time without the need to re-key the entire fact table. Suppose, for instance, we are tracking sales of a product, and the owner of a brand changes over time. In a single table model (models that flatten fact and dimensional data into a single table), expensive updates or truncating/loading would be required to update the entire table to reflect the proper brand owner. In a dimensional model, only the brand owner attribute of the product dimension needs to change. This change is then reflected to downstream reporting and analytic applications without much fanfare.

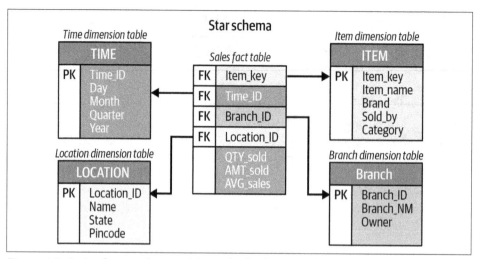

Figure 4-9. A simple star schema without slowly changing dimensions

As operational data is transformed into the star schema, careful consideration must be taken into account when choosing what is fact versus dimensional data. Design considerations of the database will have direct impact on ETL that feeds the data warehouse. For instance, data can be added to a warehouse at the transaction level, or it can be imported, transformed, and inserted in batch. Any of these approaches require ETL and proper denormalizing to fulfill data warehouse requirements—the ability to query data quickly and fulfill data requests.

Dimensional versus fact data in a streaming context

Fact and dimensional data both change state over time, but at different rates. To fully understand a customer's behavior during an online shopping instance, the data warehouse must be able to track each interaction a customer has with products, perhaps even keeping track of what the customer added to their basket, what they removed, and in what order. For a traditional data warehouse system, this poses a challenge, since each batch insert of data to the warehouse accounts for only the point in time when a snapshot was taken. But, with the advent of the Kappa architecture and the use of tiered storage, the complexities of providing real-time actionable data become simplified and achievable. Insights can now be delivered at near real time, and the data warehouse can take advantage of this in terms of data ingestion.

Dimensional data, as stated before, also changes over time. This is an important topic that often gets overlooked when building a star schema data model. These so-called slowly changing dimensions also require attention to detail, because for accurate analytics, it is important to be able to view customers, products, and locations as they were known at the time of a transaction or set of transactions. Understanding the attributes of a particular product today is important, but it is also important to understand what that product *was* six months or even a year ago. Understanding a customer's demographic profile at time of purchase is important to understanding and predicting how other customers may also behave.

Slowly changing dimensions, too, have suffered from the historical type of data warehousing ingestion that we saw in the past. Kappa architecture again simplifies the slowly changing dimension definition. Rather than materializing point-in-time information about dimensions on certain intervals, understanding what a dimension looks like at a particular point in time becomes a matter of looking at a point in time in a stream and determining its characteristics. To take this concept even further, in a streaming data mesh, the dimensions of a data model become data products, along with the fact data. This allows the data product engineer to publish a standardized interface to dimensional data that allows for point-in-time lookups. Rather than creating views based on some sort of SCD Type-6 setup, and querying this view, business logic to create point-in-time lookups now becomes encapsulated in the data product itself.

Materialized views in streams

In its simplest terms, *materialized views* are preprocessed query results stored on disk. The idea is that the preprocessing of the query is always running, so that at any time a user can query the materialized view and expect to get the latest results. Conversely, a *traditional view* is a query that is not preprocessed and is run at the time the view is queried. The results of a traditional view are not stored on disk.

Both materialized and traditional views will return the same result, except the materialized view will run faster since the results are already precomputed, while the traditional view needs to process the view first before returning the result. Since the preprocessing in a materialized view is happening in the background, it has asynchronous characteristics. Conversely, since a traditional view processes the query only on request and responds with the result, it has synchronous characteristics.

Let's take these concepts further. In "Ingesting Data Product Derivatives with Kafka Connect" on page 46, we discussed the differences between synchronous and asynchronous data sources. The primary difference is that synchronous data sources follow batching semantics, while asynchronous data sources follow streaming semantics.

This description of materialized views was explained in the context of a single database. Materialized views don't actually exist in only a single database. The materialized view semantics of preprocessing data exists when replicating data from an active instance of a database to a passive instance, as seen in Figure 4-10.

In this illustration of a disaster recovery solution, the application uses the "active" database and fails over to the "passive" database in case the active database crashes. The data passes over the write-ahead log (WAL) and "materializes" in the passive database. Every transaction that occurred in the active database is recorded in the

WAL and is executed in the passive database in the background. This replication of data therefore happens asynchronously and is an example of a materialized view involving two databases.

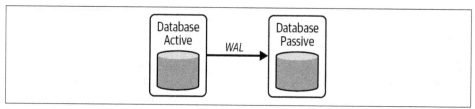

Figure 4-10. Database replication using a write-ahead log creating a materialized view in the passive database

The Debezium connector that we previously discussed actually reads the WAL of the databases it supports to capture changes, but instead of sending it to another database of the same instance, it sends it to Kafka (see Figure 4-11).

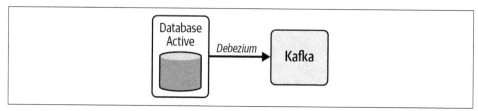

Figure 4-11. Database replication using a WAL to populate Kafka with CDC transactions

From this point, you can build multiple materialized views. As in the case in Figure 4-12, you can create a materialized view in ksqlDB or in another passive database using Flink.

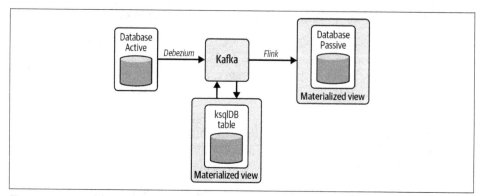

Figure 4-12. Building multiple materialized views from a single Debezium CDC connector reading from the WAL

CDC use cases are really used for models or entities that are the outcomes of DDD. These entities do not change often, so they change slowly. In ETL pipelines, these entities are the dimensional data used to enrich fact data.

Streaming ETL with domain-driven design

Let's now tie this information back to streaming ETL. In summary, dimensional data is sourced by materialized views, which are sourced by CDC streams, which are sourced from the WALs from the original source databases. We now have a fully streaming data pipeline for dimensional data that will be used to enrich fact data. It also is our solution to a fully streaming ETL, where both the dimensional data and fact data are backed by streams.

This is the goal we want: to enable streaming ETL in all domains. To accomplish this, we need two types of data products: dimensional and fact. If we were to make them streaming data products, they would be different types of streaming data products—a CDC stream for dimensional data and an append-only stream for fact data. CDC streams contain only changes captured from WALs in an operational (transactional) source database, and append-only streams contain fact data.

In DDD, the domain model defines the entities, their interrelationships, and their interactions based on business logic. Fact data is these interaction events between entities bound with time and state. Dimensional data is the *create, update, and delete* events related to entities and their interrelationships.

For example, a visitor to a website doesn't change their name often, so this is a slowly changing dimension. But they may be clicking many things around the site—adding and removing items in their cart, for example. This is fact data that arrives fast and is associated with time. Joining the fact data with the dimensional data is an ETL process that enriches fact data with dimensional data so that analysts can know who clicked, and they can infer why, when, and where the user clicked to improve their experience. Model training requires capturing dimensional state not from dimensional tables, but from enriched fact data (enriched from dimensional) so that it can capture the current state of a dimension along with time with the click event.

Publishing Data Products with AsyncAPI

We've defined the streaming data product requirements based on the requirements provided by other domains. We also identified the data product derivatives (and subscribed to other domain products if necessary). We then extracted and transformed the data to create a new data product. At this point the data product is ready for publishing into the data mesh. We will further use AsyncAPI to define the consumption point of the data product content.

AsyncAPI is an open source project created to simplify and standardize definitions of streaming data sources. AsyncAPI is an interface definition language (IDL) that lets applications written in one language interface with applications written in other languages. In this case, AsyncAPI is an IDL that defines an asynchronous API. It allows other applications to create integrations with the streaming data product agnostic to any programming language. The process of publishing a data product will involve creating an AsyncAPI YAML document and registering it to the streaming data mesh.

Registering the Streaming Data Product

AsyncAPI documents are written in YAML, a machine-readable document format that can easily be edited by a domain engineer so it is also somewhat human-readable as well. When we register a data product, we will create an AsyncAPI YAML document and register it with a streaming data catalog, which we will talk more about in Chapter 5. For now, the streaming data catalog will hold all the data products in the streaming data mesh so that data product shoppers have a single place to search for streaming data products and subscribe to them.

AsyncAPI extends OpenAPI, which is formally known as Swagger (see Figure 4-13 for details). OpenAPI is also a YAML-based IDL that describes synchronous APIs. Today, synchronous APIs are registered in API gateways, like Kong and Apigee, where API shoppers can browse and search for specific APIs based on their use cases. The goal of AsyncAPI is to apply that simple approach to asynchronous data sources as well. AsyncAPI provides us a simple way to enable self-services needed to create a good experience for all users/consumers of the streaming data mesh.

The AsyncAPI YAML document will enable us to specifically define how applications can consume the streaming data product so that we can build self-services to seamlessly create integrations between domains. This ultimately builds the mesh in the streaming data mesh. The AsyncAPI YAML document will also enable us to perform searches in the streaming data catalog, which we will cover in Chapter 5.

The AsyncAPI YAML documents are parsed by applications to generate client consumer code for domains in any programming language. These applications can do other things like generate HTML pages that can be served by a streaming data catalog. We will demonstrate this in Chapter 5. In Chapter 6, we will show how an AsyncAPI YAML service can invoke a REST API that will provision a Kafka connector to read from the Kafka topic and write to Amazon S3.

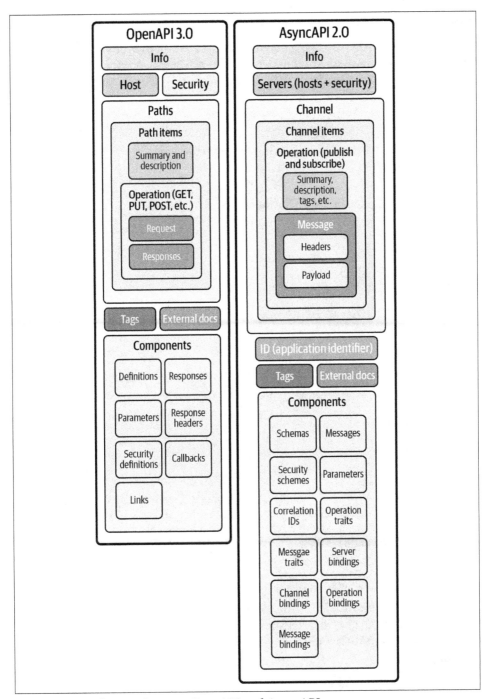

Figure 4-13. Differences between OpenAPI and AsyncAPI

Building an AsyncAPI YAML Document

Creating the AsyncAPI YAML document is the last step in publishing a data product into a streaming data mesh. Example 4-6 shows a skeleton AsyncAPI YAML document; we've removed the details. We will populate this YAML document with the metadata needed to define a streaming data product to be published to the data mesh. In YAML, all the fields are called *objects*. For instance, in Example 4-6, asyncapi, externalDocs, info, etc., are all considered objects, as well as the subobjects like covid, messages, schemas, etc. We will refer to them as objects when speaking in the context of YAML.

Example 4-6. An AsyncAPI YAML document skeleton

```
asyncapi: '2.2.0'
externalDocs:
info:
tags:
servers:
defaultContentType:
channels:
  covid:
components:
  messages:
    covidapi:
  schemas:
    covidapi:
  securitySchemes:
    user-password:
      type: userPassword
  messageTraits:
  operationTraits:
```

> The AsyncAPI example uses Confluent Cloud as the streaming platform. Confluent Cloud provides a fully managed Apache Kafka and Schema Registry, which we will talk more about in later sections of this chapter.

Objects asyncapi, externalDocs, info, and tags

Let's now build an AsyncAPI YAML document defining a streaming data product that provides COVID-19 global statistics. In Example 4-7 we populate all the descriptive information for the data product. This covers the top four sections of the YAML in Example 4-6.

Example 4-7. AsyncAPI YAML informational sections

```yaml
asyncapi: '2.2.0' ❶
externalDocs: ❷
  description: The source of the COVID-19 global statistics that is provided
  as a real-time data stream.
  url: https://covid19api.com/
info: ❸
  title: COVID-19 Global Statistics AsyncAPI Spec
  version: '0.0.1'
  description: |
    This AsyncAPI provides pub/sub information for clients to pub/sub COVID
    data to Kafka

  license:
    name: Apache 2.0
    url: https://www.apache.org/licenses/LICENSE-2.0
  contact:
    name: API Support
    url: http://www.asyncapi.com/support
    email: info@asyncapi.io
  x-twitter: '@AsyncAPISpec'

tags: ❹
  - name: root-tag1
    externalDocs:
      description: External docs description 1
      url: https://www.asyncapi.com/
  - name: root-tag2
    description: Description 2
    externalDocs:
      url: "https://www.asyncapi.com/"
  - name: root-tag3
  - name: root-tag4
    description: Description 4
  - name: root-tag5
    externalDocs:
      url: "https://www.asyncapi.com/"
```

❶ The AsyncAPI version 2.2.0.

❷ `externalDocs` provides a description of the data product and a URL where users can find more information on the data product.

❸ The `info` section of the YAML provides additional details on the data product, including version and license information.

❹ The optional `tags` section places hashtags that may relate to the data product.

Notice that in Example 4-7 we could place URLs in several places for users shopping to do further research on the data products, so it's beneficial to add them to provide all the information necessary to understand it.

Tags in this section could be used for relating data products together. This will become more useful when we start talking about knowledge graphs in Chapter 5. Knowledge graphs enable building semantic multidimensional relationships between data and metadata, making data more valuable to users.

Servers and security section

In Example 4-8 we add an important block to the YAML that provides connectivity and security information. In this case, the data product is published in a Kafka topic. AsyncAPI supports any type of streaming platform, so it needs to be configured with a `protocol` for parsers to understand how to build the integration between the streaming data product and the component that will subscribe to it.

Example 4-8. An AsyncAPI defining a data product for the data mesh

```
servers: ❶
  kafka-aws-useast2: ❷
    url: https://kafka.us-east-2.aws.confluent.cloud:9092 ❸
    protocol: kafka ❹
    description: Kafka cluster Confluent cloud AWS US-EAST-2
    security:
      - user-password: [] ❺

defaultContentType: application/json ❻
```

❶ List of servers that define the connection to the data product.

❷ `kafka-aws-useast2` is a custom property that identifies a specific Kafka server and its connection and security requirements.

❸ The URL to use to connect to the streaming platform—in this case, Apache Kafka.

❹ `protocol` identifies the type of streaming platform the data product is being served. This field informs the application reading this YAML to include specific libraries to enable connectivity to the streaming platform—in this case, Apache Kafka.

❺ `user-password` references the `securitySchema` that informs the application reading this YAML that the security mechanism to use is SASL_SSL, which ensures that the communication is encrypted and authenticated using SASL/PLAIN.

❻ The defaultContentType property informs the reading application that the content of the data product is JSON. Alternatives types could be Apache Avro or protobuf.

In Example 4-8, we have multiple options for security. Some of these are as follows:

- User and password
- Certificates
- API keys
- OAuth 2
- OpenID

The security section can contain multiple security options, but in this case there is only user-password. Most security configurations make use of user/password or certificates. In AsyncAPI, security extends OpenAPI to add other security mechanisms like OAuth 2 and OpenID that are supported by streaming platforms. We will not go over each implementation in detail because it is beyond the scope of this book (it would be a whole other book). For the purpose of this book, we will use user-password as the security mechanism. Later in this chapter we will show how we provide details for this security configuration.

Channels and topic section

Example 4-9 shows the channels block in the AsyncAPI, where a lot of the details of the streaming data product reside. Under channels is another level labeled covid that corresponds to the topic name in Apache Kafka, the topic from which the streaming data product is served. In this case, the streaming data product is again global COVID-19 statistics.

Example 4-9. channels section

```
channels:
  covid: # topic name ❶
    x-confluent-cloud-security: ❷
      $ref: '#/components/securitySchemes/user-password'
    description: Publishes/Subscribes to the COVID topic for new statistics.

    subscribe: ❸
      summary: Subscribe to global COVID-19 Statistics.
      description: |
        The schema that this service follows the https://api.covid19api.com/
      operationId: receiveNewCovidInfo
      tags: ❹
        - name: covid19api
```

```
    externalDocs:
      description: COVID-19 API
      url: https://api.covid19api.com/
  - name: covid
    description: covid service
traits: ❺
  - $ref: '#/components/operationTraits/covid'
message: ❻
  $ref: '#/components/messages/covidapi'
```

❶ The name of the channel that corresponds to the name of the Kafka topic.

❷ The security implementation. $ref property is a reference to another part of the AsyncAPI that defines the security implementation in more detail, covered in "Security schemes section" on page 80.

❸ Indicates how the client will subscribe to the covid topic. This section is for subscribers, not producers.

❹ tags allows for more relationships to be built in the knowledge graph in the streaming data catalog. We provide more metadata about the streaming data product and improved searchability.

❺ traits provides more information for the client to configure itself. In this case, AsyncAPI is referencing another part of the document that will provide more information on how the client subscriber/consumer will need to configure itself. We will go over these details in "Traits section" on page 81.

❻ message is yet another $ref that references the schema of the streaming data product. The reference points to another part of the AsyncAPI document that will give details on how the message is structured so that the client consumer can parse and process it.

The channels section of the AsyncAPI can provide both a subscribe and a publish section. We omitted the publish section because since this AsyncAPI document is meant to describe streaming data products, other domains should not have the information to produce to the Apache Kafka topic. This AsyncAPI should have only subscribers that are the other domains in the streaming data mesh.

Components section

The components object contains five subsections that hold reusable objects for different parts of the AsyncAPI specification (see Example 4-10). All objects defined within the components object will have no effect on the API unless they are explicitly referenced from properties outside the components object. In the previous sections, the AsyncAPI examples referenced many of the subsections in the components object. Let's go over each of the subsections in detail.

Example 4-10. components holds the messages and schemas details

```
components:
  messages:
  schemas:
  securitySchemes:
  messageTraits:
  operationTraits:
```

Messages section. You may recall from Example 4-9 that the channel/covid/message section of the AsyncAPI document referenced a message object that was components/messages/covidapi. That schema is defined under the components section of the AsyncAPI document. The components section contains two subsections: messages and schemas. The messages section describes the envelope of the payload (see Example 4-11), and schemas describes the payload itself.

Example 4-11. messages describes the envelope that holds the payload

```
components:
  messages:
    covidapi: ❶
      name: covidapi
      title: covid api
      summary: covidapi from https://api.covid19api.com/
      correlationId: ❷
        description: |
          You can correlate / join with other data using the
          CountryCode field.
        location: $message.payload#/CountryCode
      tags: ❸
        - name: message-tag1
          externalDocs:
            description: External docs description 1
            url: https://www.asyncapi.com/
        - name: message-tag2
          description: Description 2
          externalDocs:
            url: "https://www.asyncapi.com/"
      headers: ❹
        type: object
        properties:
          my-custom-app-header:
            type: string
          correlationId:
            type: string
```

```
    payload: ❺
      $ref: "#/components/schemas/covidapi"
    bindings: ❻
      kafka:
        key:
          type: object
          properties:
            id:
              type: string
            type:
              type: string
        bindingVersion: '0.1.0'
```

❶ The name of the message component. This is the element that is being referenced in Example 4-9.

❷ The correlationId references the (5) to identify the field to be used as a correlation ID, an identifier in message tracing. In Kafka, this will most likely be the key used to assign the partition in a topic.

❸ Again, tags can be used to build relationships between other data products or domains.

❹ The headers section provides information in the header of the message from the streaming platform. It also has the correlationId in case it is provided in the header.

❺ The payload references another section of the AsyncAPI that contains the schema of the message located in components/schemas/covidapi in the same components object.

❻ A free-form map where the keys describe the name of the protocol (in this case, the Kafka protocol), and the values describe protocol-specific definitions for the server (Kafka).

The schemas subsection shown in Example 4-12 defines the schema payload inline. *Inline* basically means that the schema is defined in the AsyncAPI YAML document. You can alternatively define the schema outside the AsyncAPI YAML document by providing a $ref, which is just a URL to the schema (see Example 4-13).

Example 4-12. Schema describes the payload that is the streaming data product itself

```
schemas:
    covidapi:
      type: object
      required:
```

```
      - CountryCode
    properties:
      Country:
        type: string
      CountryCode:
        type: string
        description: correlationId
      Date:
        type: string
      ID:
        type: string
      NewConfirmed:
        type: integer
      NewDeaths:
        type: integer
      NewRecovered:
        type: integer
      Premium:
        type: object
      Slug:
        type: string
      TotalConfirmed:
        type: integer
      TotalDeaths:
        type: integer
      TotalRecovered:
        type: integer
```

Using a tool like a schema registry to register and manage schemas is the preferred approach. The schema registry keeps track of schema versions and sometimes checks for compatibility to previous versions. Schemas are the "contract" between the producing domain and the consuming domain for streaming data products. This protects applications from changes to the schema that could break the data processing in the consuming domain. It also enforces producing domains to evolve their streaming data products in such a way that doesn't break compatibility to older versions. A schema registry falls under the federated data governance in the streaming data mesh, so we will go into more details in Chapter 5. In the AsyncAPI YAML document, it's important to know that instead of defining your schema inline, you can do it remotely with a schema registry (see Example 4-13).

Example 4-13. messages describes the envelope that holds the payload

```
messages:
  covidapi:
    name: covidapi
    title: covidapi
    summary: COVID 19 global statistics
    contentType: avro/binary
    schemaFormat: application/vnd.apache.avro+json;version=1.9.0
```

```
payload:
    $ref: 'http://schema-registry:8081/subjects/topic/versions/1/#covidapi' ❶
```

❶ The payload schema is an external reference to a schema registry.

Security schemes section. AsyncAPI provides specific security information in the securitySchemes object of the YAML document. Example 4-14 shows how to connect to the streaming platform, which in this case is Kafka as defined in the servers section of the AsyncAPI YAML. The description object has a property description that is provided to the consuming application. This provides more detailed information to the streaming data product client. Authors of the AsyncAPI YAML document can format the content of the description object to provide more information that AsyncAPI YAML doesn't provide.

Example 4-14. Security schemes section of components that shows more details in the description

```
securitySchemes:
    user-password:
      type: userPassword
      description: |
        Provide your Confluent KEY as the user and SECRET as the password.

        ```prop
        # Kafka
        bootstrap.servers=kafka.us-east-2.aws.confluent.cloud:9092
        security.protocol=SASL_SSL
        sasl.mechanisms=PLAIN
        sasl.username={{ CLUSTER_API_KEY }} ❶
        sasl.password={{ CLUSTER_API_SECRET }} ❷

        # Best practice for higher availability in librdkafka clients prior to 1.7
        session.timeout.ms=45000

        # Confluent Cloud Schema Registry
        schema.registry.url=https://schema-registry.westus2.azure.confluent.cloud
        basic.auth.credentials.source=USER_INFO
        basic.auth.user.info={{ SR_API_KEY }}:{{ SR_API_SECRET }} ❸
        ```

        Copy the above YAML replacing the KEY/SECRETS for both the cluster and
        schema registry and use in your Kafka clients.
```

❶ {{ CLUSTER_API_KEY }} is the key or user in user-password to use to connect to Kafka in Confluent Cloud.

❷ `{{ CLUSTER_API_SECRET }}` is the secret or password `user-password` to use to connect to Kafka in Confluent Cloud.

❸ `{{ SR_API_KEY }}`:`{{ SR_API_SECRET }}` is the key/secret or `user-password` to use when requesting schemas from the Schema Registry in Confluent Cloud.

When domain consumers want to consume a streaming data product, such as the COVID-19 global statistics data described in this AsyncAPI, they have to request access to it. Then the streaming data product manager needs to approve the requesting domain. Part of this approval may involve sending the credentials to the requesting domain so that it can put that information in its configuration to start consuming the streaming data product. In Example 4-14, this would correspond to the parameters listed in (1), (2), and (3). These parameters will need to be replaced with the credentials provided by the producing domain to gain access to the streaming data products.

The description in Example 4-14 shows specifically how to configure a consumer to read from Confluent Cloud. The client will only need to again replace the parameters with the credentials, read this configuration into the application, and pass it to the Kafka client libraries to configure it to read from Kafka. In later chapters we will demonstrate how to use the AsyncAPI YAML document to build Apache Kafka connectors instead, creating applications that read from Apache Kafka.

 It's important to remember that this example uses the user/password methodology for security. As mentioned earlier, other supported security methodologies have their own types of credentials and may not use the user/password approach. Those other security methodologies are outside the scope of this book.

Traits section. In AsyncAPI, `traits` provides additional information that could be applied to an object in the YAML document. Traits are usually used only when the application parsing the AsyncAPI YAML document is trying to generate client code in a specific language. Example 4-9 had an object called `operationId` with the value `receiveNewCovidInfo`. An application that reads an AsyncAPI YAML document called *AsyncAPI Generator* can be downloaded from the AsyncAPI website (*https://oreil.ly/dw863*). This will generate Java Spring client code for domains to compile and deploy. This application can consume the streaming data product from the streaming platform defined in the `servers` section in the AsyncAPI YAML. In this case, it will be Apache Kafka. AsyncAPI Generator will use the value in `operationId` as the method name in the source code. The traits in both `messageTraits` and `operation Traits` in Example 4-15 are used to assign values to methods like the `groupID` or `clientId` to help with generating client code.

Example 4-15. Traits are used by code generators to assign values to properties, name classes, and methods in the generated code

```
messageTraits:
  commonHeaders:
    headers:
      type: object
      properties: ❶
        my-app-header:
          type: integer
          minimum: 0
          maximum: 100
        correlationId:
          type: string

operationTraits:
  covid:
    bindings:
      kafka: ❷
        groupId: my-app-group-id-pub
        clientId: my-app-client-id-pub
        bindingVersion: '0.1.0'
```

❶ Provides more information on what headers could be used by the client for processing the streaming data product

❷ Provides binding information to Kafka that will help identify the consumer groups and elastically scale the client application if needed

Assigning Data Tags

Data tags are a simple way of providing the consuming domains with more information about the streaming data product: how it was built and what to expect when consuming it. Many of the streaming data characteristics are hard to measure, like quality and security, so it's sometimes tough to provide that important information to the consuming domain. Instead of providing a number or a score, we can provide tags that represent levels of quality and security. In this section we'll try to assign data tags to the data.

Tags can provide information about the quality or security of the streaming data product. Sometimes consuming domains want streaming data products that were unchanged (in raw form) from the original source. Other consuming domains may want that same streaming data product to be of highest quality that satisfies the format standards and security requirements. These would end up being two distinct streaming data products. Tags give us an easy way to present streaming data products to the consuming domains.

Quality

Quality is a hard characteristic to score, but we could use tags like those defined in Table 4-8.

Table 4-8. Possible quality tags

Tags	Definition
RAW	Raw data from the original source
STANDARD	Transformation to meet format standards
ENRICHED	Transformation to format standards and enrichment

For the two streaming data products originating from the same source data but with differing quality, we could assign RAW as the data quality tag for the streaming data product that serves raw data. We could also assign ENRICHED as the data quality tag for the second streaming data product, where consumers are expecting enrichment. Consuming domains would easily identify which streaming data product to request access to.

These tags could be assigned to `tags` in the AsyncAPI and domain consumers could click into it and get the tags definitions, as in Example 4-16.

Example 4-16. Adding quality tags to provide additional information

```
covidapi:
  name: covidapi
  title: covid api
  tags:
    - name: quality.RAW  ❶
      externalDocs:
        description: Provides raw source data
        url: https://somewhere/quality/raw
```

❶ `quality.RAW` corresponds to raw data. The URL would direct the domain consumer to more information on how the quality was implemented.

Security

Security in this context of informational data tags would involve protecting sensitive information in the streaming data product. Similarly to quality, security tags could also be defined as in Table 4-9.

Table 4-9. Possible security tags

Tags	Definition
FILTERED	The sensitive data was filtered or selected out of the streaming data product, or there was no sensitive information in the payload.
TOKENIZED	The sensitive data was tokenized and can be retrieved via a lookup mechanism.
ENCRYPTED	The sensitive data, was encrypted and decrypting the data to its original value requires a key.

Similarly to the tags for informing quality, the tags for security are added. You can add multiple tags to the AsyncAPI YAML document for both quality and security (Example 4-17).

Example 4-17. Adding security tags to provide additional information

```
covidapi:
  name: covidapi
  title: covid api
  tags:
    - name: security.FILTERED ❶
      externalDocs:
        description: Provides raw source data
        url: https://somewhere/security/filtered
```

❶ `security.FILTERED` means that if any of the information was sensitive, it was filtered or omitted from the final streaming data product.

Example 4-17 shows how we can provide information to the consuming domain about what was done to the data to be secured. The `url` is an additional resource that could provide more information about what was filtered out and why.

Throughput

Providing throughput to the streaming data product will provide very important scalability information to the consuming domain. *Throughput* can be measured in megabytes per second (MBps). It is an indicator of how fast the data is coming to a consuming domain. Some streaming data products can be slow, like the slowly changing dimensional data discussed in "Dimensional versus fact data in a streaming context" on page 66. Other streaming data can be really fast, like clickstream data from a web application or a Twitter feed.

Similarly to quality and security, in Example 4-18 you could provide the throughput as a description in a throughput tag and a URL that will provide additional information about how the Apache Kafka topic is configured to enable that level of throughput, like the number of partitions.

Example 4-18. Describing throughput in AsyncAPI

```
subscribe:
    summary: Subscribe to global COVID 19 Statistics.
    description: |
        The schema that this service follows the https://api.covid19api.com/
    operationId: receiveNewCovidInfo
    tags:
      - name: throughput ❶
        externalDocs:
          description: 10/mbps ❷
          url: https://localhost/covid119/throughput ❸
```

❶ Throughput tag

❷ The tag description that provides the throughput value

❸ A URL where consuming domains can find out more about how the throughput is implemented

Versioning

It is important to provide the version of the streaming data product. This allows consuming domains to understand whether the streaming data product is ready for their production workloads or whether a major version change has occurred that they could take advantage of.

Example 4-19 shows how AsyncAPI can provide detailed versioning information to consuming domains they could use when managing their own application development.

Example 4-19. AsyncAPI YAML informational sections

```
info:
  title: COVID 19 Global Statistics AsyncAPI Spec
  version: '0.0.1'
  description: |
    This streaming data product is in preview. DISCLAIMER - this streaming data
    product could implement breaking changes. Do not use this for your production
    applications in your domain.
  contact:
    name: API Support
    url: http://www.asyncapi.com/support
```

It may also be beneficial if the change log to updated versions is provided either in the description or a URL. This includes any changes to the ETL data pipeline that produces the data product and any changes in the original source.

Data derivatives that originate from other streaming data products from other domains should be identified as well in tags or URLs so that consuming domains can recursively drill down into the sources that compose the final streaming data product. In later chapters, we will go over ways to do this.

Monitoring

Monitoring information about the streaming data product is also critical for consuming domains to see. This again could be provided as yet another URL or tag in the AsyncAPI YAML document. Table 4-10 shows some of the important information that consuming domains would want to know.

Table 4-10. Information that could be learned from monitoring streaming data products

Information	Insight
Number of consumers	• Indicates the popularity of the streaming data product. • To see which other domains are consuming this data.
Error count/SLA	• To get the current status of the streaming data product in case the consuming domain is experiencing issues. This will answer questions like: — Is it active? — Is there a current outage? — When will the streaming data product expected to be back online? • To see if the streaming data product is meeting uptime SLA.
Throughput/bandwidth	• To see if the streaming data product is at maximum capacity.

If the consuming domain requires 99.999% for its own applications and the streaming data product provides only 99.9%, it may want to request higher SLA guarantees, which may result in a separate streaming data product.

Consuming domains will want to set up alerts to these metrics so that they can react to potential issues. You can provide better data mesh experience if you provide monitoring to all your streaming data products and have them be programmatically consumable or alertable to the consuming domains.

Summary

In this chapter, we outlined all the necessary steps to build a streaming data product: how to define requirements, ingestion, transformation, and ultimately publishing an AsyncAPI YAML document. We did all this with the skill set of generalist engineers that we expect from domain engineers: JSON, SQL, and YAML. This AsyncAPI document will allow us to build a streaming data mesh. In Chapter 5, we will talk about how we can use the AsyncAPI YAML document to populate a streaming data catalog. We will also use AsyncAPI applications (tools) that will generate HTML pages in a streaming data catalog application and see how we can extend it to add a streaming data mesh workflow. In later chapters, we will continue to use the AsyncAPI document to build self-services that can build integrations and retrieve metadata recursively, such as data lineage.

CHAPTER 5

Federated Computational Data Governance

Governance provides the interoperability and controls to allow domains to work together while protecting each one from unwanted activity. Moreover, data governance in a streaming data mesh provides a centralized, distributed way to manage domain operations, metadata, and service definitions. That is what we will focus on when defining policies and controls in a streaming data mesh.

The federated data governance in a streaming data mesh is tasked to create a harmonious community of domains sharing data with one another while maintaining domain autonomy.

Chapter 1 discussed the idea of having multiple meshes within a streaming data mesh—meshes that stretch beyond data. One of these is a mesh for streaming data governance. This idea of a data governance mesh is similar to the state and federal governance relationship we see in society today. A state or local government has autonomy over a certain region, whereas the federal government provides overarching policies that impact operations at the state and local level. The goal of this relationship is to create harmonious communities. The same applies to a streaming data mesh. We can think of state and local governments as domains that control the data governance only within the bounds of their domain, while the federated computational data governance is akin to the federal government that enforces policies that maintain harmony between domains.

Computational in federated computational data governance means the rules and policies that support data governance are implemented as self-services or automation. Self-services and automation are written in code, built by engineers supporting the mesh, whom we've been calling the centralized engineers, or the centralized team.

In this chapter we will outline the important principles of data governance in general and identify ownership of the authority to administer these principles in a streaming data mesh. We will also cover the computational aspect of data governance as it relates to a streaming data mesh.

 The name *federated computational data governance* is a lot to write and say. To simplify, we call it just *data governance* with the assumption that it is computational. We call the overarching data governance, *federal data governance*. Likewise for the domains: *domain data governance*.

In this chapter we'll go over some foundations on data governance and apply them to streaming data governance. Then we will talk about the importance of metadata streaming data products and what it should compose. We'll go over some tools that make managing metadata easier and could be included in a streaming data mesh. Lastly, we'll go over the roles that aid with data governance.

Data Governance in a Streaming Data Mesh

Data governance is a set of policies, standards, processes, roles, and responsibilities that collectively ensure accountability and ownership of data across the business. *Policies* are the rules and regulations surrounding data defined by the business itself or, more importantly, externally by laws that, if broken, could cost a business a massive amount in fines. These policies also include enforcement of *standards* that enable interoperability and consumability of data between domains, especially in a decentralized data platform like a streaming data mesh. These policies are implemented as *processes* and controls on data by authorizing, authenticating, and safeguarding private or personal data. Policies are implemented using *roles* that represent groups, people, or systems to create access controls around data.

Data Lineage Graph

All the data governance information—policies, standards, processes, and roles—can be aggregated into a *data lineage* graph. Data lineage provides the entire history of the data: origin, transformations, enrichments, users who engineered the transformations, etc. Consumers of the data need to trust that the data they will be using is the correct data. Data lineage provides a perspective that creates trust. It does so by mapping out the steps for policies, standards, processes, roles, and responsibilities that were involved with the sourcing, transformation, enrichment, and cleansing of the data.

In Figure 5-1 data governance policies are clearly identified as "Filter for GDPR" and "Cleanse for standardizing." The callouts on the lineage also identify the domain and engineer who published and assembled the data product, respectively.

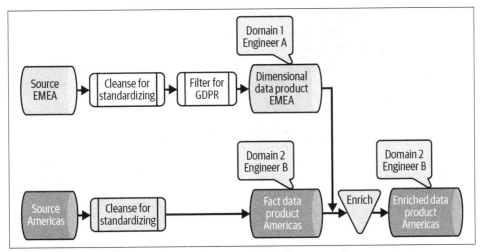

Figure 5-1. Example lineage graph identifying steps that cover data governance

Data governance in a streaming data mesh should satisfy these requirements:

- When data is in motion, domains need to be extra careful that protected data isn't breaking any regulations that may cost them a lot in fines and customer trust. Domains need to identify the regulations that affect the streaming data products and provide domain tools that will make it easy to safeguard protected data.

- Since domains will be sharing data among themselves, there needs to be a set of standards that promote interoperability. To do this, there will need to be a way to define data models using schemas so that domains can easily define and consume these standards programmatically.

- Defining roles or groups of users in a streaming data mesh is critical in helping safeguard protected data. For example, a whole domain could fall into a single group name. This will make it easier for streaming data product owners to grant or drop access to their domain data.

- Domain engineers who build streaming data products need simple ways to obfuscate protected data. For example, they need simple tools that allow them to encrypt data before it leaves their domain. Conversely, consuming domains need a way to decrypt that same data. Similarly, domain engineers need an ability to tokenize/detokenize data.

- Domain engineers need a way to easily build data lineage that spans multiple domains. They need to preserve detailed source information and transformations related to standardizations and security.

Data governance in a streaming data mesh requires data steward responsibility, which is essentially the same as the data product owner provides. The data product owner is accountable for the data products in the domain and is responsible for maintaining quality, accessibility, and security for the data products within the domain, along with its metadata. This creates a high level of transparency that consumers rely upon and is part of a good streaming data product.

Streaming Data Catalog to Organize Data Products

A *streaming data catalog* is an application that organizes an inventory of data and its metadata in an enterprise to enable their discovery and governance. This is applicable to streaming data products and provides a one-stop shop for domains to search and subscribe to streaming data in a streaming data mesh. It provides all the metadata that describes how the data was prepared, how it is formatted, its origins, and the security and regulations it enforces. In a streaming data mesh, streaming data catalogs should showcase to the user not just the data itself but also the scalability limits of the data product (computational limits, etc.).

In the next sections, we will discuss components that make up metadata for streaming data products that are published. We will discuss how to capture this data so that it isn't lost. And ultimately, we will compile all these components into a federated model so that this metadata can be shared across the streaming data mesh.

Metadata

Metadata is a term that is often overloaded to encompass many different usages. Commonly defined as "data about data," metadata in terms of a data platform refers to information containing the following:

- Tables definitions, column names, descriptions, and relationships
- Validation rules for data assets
- Data types
- Data owner
- Lineage information, including source and transformation(s) applied

The metadata that comes with a streaming data product should provide enough information for domains to understand where the data came from, how it was put together, and how it is secured. We'll use a metaphor to help make this clearer: data products are like products in a grocery store. When shopping, we want assurance that the product is from a trusted manufacturer and contains ingredients compatible with our consumption needs. We are also assured that the product was manufactured in a safe and trusted location, packaged in a manner that guarantees that the product has not been tampered with, and the product's shelf life has not expired. Metadata about data products is no different.

Understanding what has been done to the streaming data product shows transparency and trust. Many corporate environments tend to have multiple "copies" of data, often with similar content, that are maintained by completely different teams. This often leads to discrepancies in departmental reports since the one single source of truth, while it may exist, is not understood or utilized by all teams. Data products solve this problem by creating a single source for enterprise and extra-enterprise information—a governed data source that has common content and, more importantly, common metadata.

When metadata is maintained and published, as in the products of a streaming data mesh, users within the enterprise are able to discover the proper source of data for their uses, understand the descriptive information about the data, interpret any transformations that may have happened along the way, and apply proper usage of data by understanding proper data types. If there is an issue with the definition of data, this can be brought to the attention of the product owner, and its content can be corrected in a sprint cycle or feature request to avoid data fragmentation and duplication of efforts.

Metadata is no different from slowly changing dimensional data and should be treated as such. In a streaming data mesh, metadata must be published as a data product itself. Its definitions must be globally consumable by users of data products, as well as consumable by other data products making use of other data products in data enrichment and enhancement. As metadata changes, its impacts must be available in real time so that all data products remain in sync. For this reason, a streaming data product that exposes metadata for all data products in a domain is a requirement. This requirement can be created with the same streaming technology on which the streaming data mesh is built.

In this section we will talk about four categories of metadata: schemas, lineage, security, and scalability. All four provide enough metadata for our streaming data products to gain trust from domain consumers.

Schemas

In Chapter 3 we introduced domain-driven design and highlighted its ability to help business experts and engineers build domain models. These models naturally help expose entities that in turn become data products within a domain. These domain entities and events are defined with schemas that become the basis for rules around the structure and security of the data. These rules eventually become the business-driven policies for data governance.

Suppose we defined an entity called Employee during the DDD phase (see Figure 5-2). For simplicity, we care only about the properties: ID, SSN, first name, last name, and address.

Figure 5-2. An employee entity that was defined during the DDD phase

Example 5-1 would be the corresponding JSON schema that encodes the entity that can be processed by tools and applications.

Example 5-1. A JSON schema that defines an Employee domain entity

```
{
    "$schema": "https://json-schema.org/draft/2020-12/schema",
    "$id": "https://example.com/product.schema.json",
    "title": "Employee",
    "description": "An employee in your company",
    "type": "object",
    "properties": {
        "empid": {
            "description": "Identifier that is not a SSN",
            "type": "integer"
        },
        "SSN": {
            "description": "SSN",
            "type": "string"
        }
        ,
        "fname": {
            "description": "First name",
            "type": "string"
        },
        "lname": {
            "description": "Last name",
            "type": "string"
        },
        "address": {
            "description": "Address",
            "type": "string"
        }
    },
    "required": [
        "empid", "SSN", "fname", "lname", "address"
```

```
    ]
}
```

 The Employee domain entity contains many examples of PII. As we build data products around this entity, we will have to ensure that these elements are properly handled so that we do not unintentionally disclose sensitive information. Later in the chapter we will discuss ways to properly handle this type of information, both from a security and data governance perspective, so that data products properly handle PII as well as PHI.

Lineage

Data lineage is the path the data took from its source origin, the stops it made along the way, and its destination. This includes information on all the systems it passed through, how it was cleansed, what it was enriched with, and how it was secured. Capturing all that metadata is difficult because many of those systems and applications don't share information. It's up to you to assemble the data's path by pulling metadata from all those systems/applications and assembling them in hopes that you find the path your data took from its current location (destination) to its source system. Lineage is probably the hardest piece of metadata to acquire for either streaming or batching data pipelines.

OpenLineage is an open source lineage platform that tracks metadata about ETL applications. It gives domains a way to build a lineage without having to assemble heaps of metadata. It has REST, Java, and Python APIs for applications to submit start and end ETL jobs. It's a way to collect, aggregate, and visualize data pipelines in a single application.

OpenLineage uses a tool called Marquez for its user interface and lineage repository, as seen in Figure 5-3. Notice also that OpenLineage is best suited for batch processes, but you can define runs that can be streaming ETL jobs.

You can invoke the OpenLineage API at each step of the streaming data pipeline to add to the streaming ETL lineage all the way up to the consuming domain. In Figure 5-4 you can see how the lineage graph starts to build up as more components are added to it by streaming data pipelines.

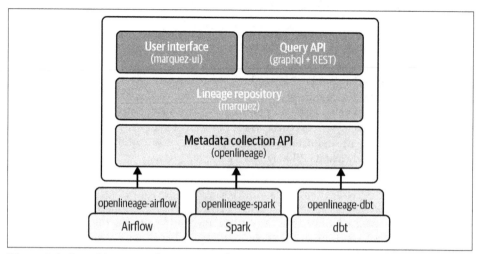

Figure 5-3. OpenLineage architecture stack

Figure 5-4. OpenLineage showing an example of a lineage diagram

When invoking OpenLineage APIs, ensure that you provide enough metadata for domains to get a full understanding of how the data is being transformed and enriched in the streaming process. For instance:

- Provide enough information for domains to fully identify the system(s) from which the streaming data product was derived, including all related applications using or creating the data.

- Identify the fields that were tokenized or encrypted, and identify how to derive or look up the original value.

- Identify fields that were filtered out, and reasons for the omission.

- Include the information for other streaming data products from other domains that were used as derivatives so that OpenLineage can build the entire lineage graph that extends beyond the bounds of your domain.

- At each step of the streaming pipeline, provide the associated schema and how it enriched or transformed the data.

- If possible, provide contacts for each step so that consuming domains have a way to inquire about implementations or issues.

In the GitHub repository (*https://oreil.ly/Go_6E*) for this book, you will be able to run OpenLineage using Docker and build your own lineage graph using the examples provided in the repository.

Unfortunately, most stream processing engines do not support OpenLineage integration. In these cases, you will need to invoke the OpenLineage APIs as part of your CI/CD process to send START and COMPLETE events. This will build the lineage graph and page that can be referenced in the streaming data product page generated from AsyncAPI, which we will cover in "Generating the Data Product Page from AsyncAPI" on page 98.

Security

Security information is often insufficient or even omitted from metadata. Many businesses have a global footprint, and moving data globally would eventually be subject to data privacy regulations like GDPR. Similarly, if the data is health-care related, it is subject to regulations defined by HIPAA. Providing information on how streaming data products handle regulations is critical, so that domains can maintain compliance.

For example, when being audited, domains must know which fields are considered private, where the process ran to protect that private data, and how it was implemented. This information could easily be provided in the lineage graph. An auditor can just traverse the graph to see where the data originated and how it was protected. This is especially important when a business has multiple domains in global regions. There should be proof that we practice transitive data protections and permissions through domains.

Information on access to data is also important. Some domains should not have private data. The lineage graph should show private data being filtered out for those domains. Other domains that do have access should have a way to derive the private data because it should not travel unprotected.

Role-based access control (RBAC) is a model to restrict access to data. Similarly, attribute-based access control (ABAC) restricts access at the field level. RBAC and ABAC make organizing accessibility to data easier to understand and implement. Access *roles* in the metadata provide increased trustability. Most streaming platforms have some level of access control as well as an API to query the access rules already defined.

All the metadata from different systems that describe the streaming data product creates the data governance "mesh" we spoke about in earlier chapters. The metadata from this mesh of data governance tools needs to be accumulated to a single view for the domains to see. In the next section, we will walk through how we can aggregate this metadata and build a streaming data product view to be deployed into a streaming data catalog.

Scalability

It's not enough to provide metadata about the streaming data product itself. It's also necessary to provide metadata around how it's being served and the guarantees it comes with.

In Chapter 4 we stressed that scalability needs to be considered early, at ingestion of the data derivatives. That scalability propagates to the final streaming data product. Preserving that information allows data consumers to have a good understanding of the data product's scalability. Information such as the throughput, in megabytes per second (MBps), and the number of partitions, should be included with the metadata.

You should also provide metadata about usage statistics. Domain consumers can see how many existing consumers are reading the data product. They will be able to tell if the data product is at maximum serving capacity and if they need to request more from the data product owner. They can also see how many outages occurred in the past year to get an idea of its uptime guarantees.

All four of these categories should be provided with the streaming data product. In Chapter 4 we used AsyncAPI tags in the YAML document to help users provide more metadata around the streaming data product. Next, we will generate a data catalog page that will describe the streaming data product and provide links to the additional metadata.

Generating the Data Product Page from AsyncAPI

In Chapter 4 we generated an AsyncAPI YAML document that defines streaming data products. Since AsyncAPI can be extended, all the metadata we accumulate for our data products can be used to populate or be referenced in the AsyncAPI. In this section we will show you how to generate an HTML page using the AsyncAPI YAML document, populating it with the information that domains want to see about your data products.

In this book's GitHub repository (*https://oreil.ly/Go_6E*) examples are committed for you to clone from Example 5-2.

Example 5-2. The git command to clone the corresponding GitHub repository

```
git clone https://github.com/hdulay/streaming-data-mesh.git
```

Example 5-3 contains the command to generate HTML from an AsyncAPI YAML document.

Example 5-3. Generating HTML from an AsyncAPI YAML document

```
cd chapter5
ag \ ❶
    ../kafka-pubsub.yaml \ ❷
    https://github.com/hdulay/streaming-data-mesh/tree/main/html-template \ ❸
    -o output \ ❹
    --force-write ❺
```

❶ ag is the AsyncAPI generator: a command-line tool that can be downloaded locally and executed to generate outputs from AsyncAPI YAML documents.

❷ The AsyncAPI YAML document for ag to use.

❸ The template that is used by ag—in this case, to generate HTML.

❹ -o identifies the output directory to place the HTML files.

❺ --force-write overwrites any previously generated HTML files.

The output of the command looks like Figure 5-5. The page consists of all the streaming data products entered in the AsyncAPI YAML. This HTML page can be used to publish into a streaming data catalog. Alternatively, the catalog could use AsyncAPI plug-ins to generate the HTML page dynamically from an AsyncAPI YAML document.

Figure 5-5. AsyncAPI-generated HTML

In Figure 5-5 three buttons were added to show how we could embed a streaming data mesh workflow into the HTML. A streaming data mesh workflow defines how users can request access and ultimately start consuming streaming data products. Understand that you have complete control of how this HTML document is generated and can conform to a workflow that meets the needs of your business. The data product consumer can click the Request Access button to request access to the data product. Both the Create Connector and Create Spring Client buttons are ways the data product consumer can subscribe to the streaming data product and pull it into their domain after the request has been approved. A suggestion for a streaming data mesh workflow will be covered in "Access Workflow" on page 101.

At the time of this writing, no open source data catalogs can use AsyncAPI as a way to publish streaming data products. Many companies have built their own data catalogs that can support streaming data products. Alternatively, since AsyncAPI extends OpenAPI, which is a specification for defining synchronous restful APIs, we can use existing OpenAPI registries like Apicurio to publish our streaming data products.

Apicurio Registry

Apicurio_ is an open source registry that stores artifacts (files). It provides the ability to add, update, and remove these artifacts from the store via REST APIs. The artifacts it supports are OpenAPI, AsyncAPI, GraphQL, Apache Avro, Google Protocol Buffers, JSON Schema, Kafka Connect schema, WSDL, and XML Schema (XSD).

Apicurio also can be used as a schema registry, which we will talk more about later in this chapter. For now we will use it to register our AsyncAPI YAML documents as a way to publish our streaming data products. In the GitHub repository, we use Docker to run Apicurio and register our AsyncAPI YAML document. Figure 5-6 shows the page in Apicurio after the AsyncAPI has been loaded.

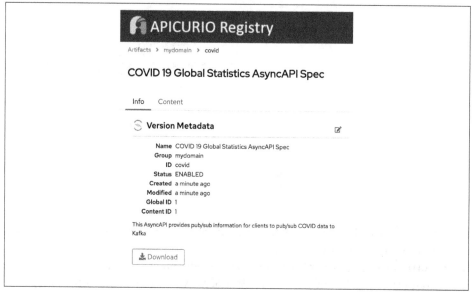

Figure 5-6. Apicurio after the AsyncAPI YAML was registered

In Apicurio, domains can search for data products by name, group, description, labels, global ID, and content ID. They can subsequently contact the domain with the email found under Content.

Access Workflow

Figure 5-5 was generated by an AsyncAPI HTML generator that adds buttons to the page: Request Access, Create Connector, and Create Spring Client. They hint at a possible workflow where users requests access, the data product owner grants access and sends access credentials, and then users use those credentials to consume the data into their domain either by a connector or a Spring client (see Figure 5-7). Businesses can include additional workflow steps to satisfy their data governance requirements.

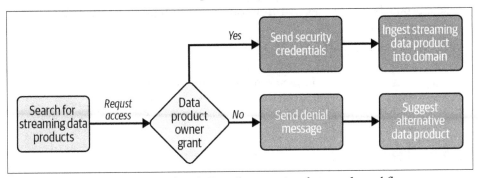

Figure 5-7. AsyncAPI-generated HTML with streaming data mesh workflow

Organizing the tasks, like granting access requests, could be confusing. In the next section we'll try to do this.

Centralized Versus Decentralized

Roles and their tasks need to be designated as either *federal* (centralized) or *domain* (decentralized). Some tasks and roles are easy to assign, but others are not and may overlap both centralized and decentralized teams. In this section we'll try to provide some delineation.

Centralized Engineers

Centralized engineers are specialized to build the self-services the domains will use to build and publish streaming data products.

These centralized engineers are also responsible for maintaining and managing the metadata and security for all the domains and their streaming data products.

This metadata includes the following:

Streaming data catalog
> Where all the streaming data products are registered and where domains can search for them.

Schema registry
> Where domains register their schemas, but schema evolution is controlled by the centralized team.

OpenLineage
> Where entire lineage graphs can be centrally assembled, allowing them to be linked between domains. This is critical when domains are building streaming data products that are derived from other streaming data products from other domains.

Security tasks include include:

- Integrating systems that authenticate users to the streaming data mesh like Lightweight Directory Access Protocol (LDAP) and single sign-on (SSO)
- Enabling encryption between the domains

Decentralized (Domain) Engineers

The decentralized engineers are the domain engineers. These engineers usually are application engineers and may have little to no knowledge of data engineering. They require tools to source, build, and publish streaming data products without much coding. Low-code and easy configuration are the expectations of these engineers so they can focus more on the applications that power the business.

These engineers should know their domain model well enough to understand what would make a good streaming data product. They define the schemas that represent their data. But they do not completely control the way they should evolve. Schema evolution should be controlled by a schema registry managed by the centralized team. The schema registry will force domains to evolve their schemas to ensure compatibility to the domains already consuming their streaming data products without breaking.

Domain engineers also control the authorization (or access) to their streaming data products. They should know if providing their data to other domains will break regulations like GDPR or HIPAA. They will need deny access to domains that should not subscribe to their data, or offer another that has been filtered, tokenized, or encrypted. Granting permissions to streaming data products should already be built into the streaming platform and are typically implemented as ACLs or rRBACs.

Domain engineers should have all the tools and services available to them to be able to perform all these tasks.

Summary

In this chapter we mentioned there isn't a data catalog that follows the access workflow we've defined. Alternatively, you may be able to extend existing streaming data catalogs to hold the access workflow. Otherwise, you'll need to build a data catalog that supports the access workflow from scratch with these requirements:

- Support views for different roles: data product engineer, data product owner, data product consumer.

- Be able to consume AsyncAPI YAML documents when domains register a new or updated streaming data product.

- Support requests for access workflow to streaming data products.

All other data governance tools that provide the additional metadata needed for streaming data products are listed in Table 5-1.

Table 5-1. Data governance tools summary

Tool	Usage
Apicurio, as a streaming data catalog	We used Apicurio as a temporary streaming data catalog for our AsyncAPI. Since it's open source software, it could be extended to be a streaming data catalog by adding the requirements stated previously. It also has a built-in schema registry with version compatibility support.
Confluent Schema Registry	This tool registers schemas with built-in compatibility support. It also supports JSON, Avro, and protobuf schemas.
Karapace	This is an open source version of Confluent's Schema Registry.
OpenLineage (Marquez)	The data lineage tracker that can span multiple domains.
Application performance management, like Datadog, AppDynamics, New Relic, Prometheus, Grafana	This is software that enables the observation and analysis of application health and user experience. Prometheus and Grafana are both open source tools for metric data collection and metric visualizations.

As we mentioned earlier, the centralized engineers build the self-services that support streaming data governance. They also support all centralized services like publishing and requesting access to streaming data products. In Chapter 6 we will discuss all the self-services you'll need to support the domains in a streaming data mesh.

Self-Service Data Infrastructure

Chapter 1 described self-service infrastructures. We said they are the "easy buttons" that make data product engineering simpler for domains. These easy buttons hide the hard parts behind a streaming data mesh. It is the responsibility of the central team to implement the hard parts behind the easy buttons.

In this chapter, we will list the self-services we will need in a streaming data mesh. We will focus on the names and signature of the self-services (their names and request/ response arguments). We will save the discussion on how these self-services will be implemented for Chapter 7.

Self-services are the interfaces (or APIs) that domains see and use when working with a streaming data mesh. There should be a self-service for every function that a domain needs to develop and deploy streaming data products.

 The terms *service* and *self-service* are used a lot in this book. We use *self-service* to indicate the interface that faces the domains. The term *service* refers to any generic service. We will try to avoid referring to self-services as services.

Theself-services described in this chapter will be CLIs that are executed from a terminal. We do this strictly for convenience. These same self-services can be implemented as RESTful services or a web interface. An example CLI can be found in the GitHub repository (*https://oreil.ly/Go_6E*).

The self-services we define are also designed to ensure that all security requirements, data governance requirements, and general best practices are followed. Since domains normally will not know how to properly configure any of the resources they will be using, these self-services will automatically configure them. This includes configurations for security and data governance.

When building self-services, don't ask the domains how many brokers they want. They will not and should not know the answer. Instead ask them, "Do you want an extra-small, small, medium, large, or extra-large streaming platform?" You could also , "How many data products do you expect to publish?" or even "How many consuming domains do you expect?" These questions should map to the size and capacity of the resource the self-service will build.

The best approach to building self-services for domains is to follow what many SaaS services do. They follow a serverless model that is easier for their users to understand and utilize in their applications. The intention of the serverless SaaS providers is to not require their users to worry about the "servers" that are allocated on their behalf. Users can focus more on their business rather than managing and tuning servers. This should be the same model for self-services: to make a streaming data mesh serverless so domains need to focus only on their business.

Self-services can be divided into two major categories: services related to resources and services related to data governance. In this chapter, we will use the CLI model to help you understand how a domain can easily interface with a streaming data mesh while keeping the serverless approach.

Throughout this chapter, you will see the help information for the CLI commands (indicated by the -h argument after each command). The information displayed shows additional subcommands and arguments that are either optional or required.

Streaming Data Mesh CLI

Let's begin with the *login* command in Example 6-1. The domain engineer or data product owner (which we'll refer to as *domain personas*) will log in to the streaming data mesh. This creates the security credentials and domain configuration, saved in a hidden folder on the domain persona's operating system. All subsequent commands can then look up that information for convenience. Here, sdm.py is a CLI that allows domain personas to interact with the streaming data mesh.

Example 6-1. Logging in to the streaming data mesh

```
$ ./cli/sdm.py login
You have successfully logged into the streaming data mesh. Your credentials
have been stored in ~/.streaming-data-mesh/auth.
```

Example 6-2 shows all the commands available for the domain persona to use. Each command has a description provided next to it. The resource-related commands are cluster, connect, and streaming. The commands related to data governance are access, users, login, and logout. The version command is informational only, providing the version of the CLI.

Example 6-2. Available commands in the CLI

```
$ ./cli/sdm.py -h
Usage:
  streaming-data-mesh.sh [tool]

Available Commands:
  domain      Manage domain.
  cluster     Manage streaming platform.
  connect     Manage connect cluster.
  streaming   Manage stream processing platform.
  access      Manage access to resources.
  users       Manage domain users.
  login       Log into the streaming data mesh.
  logout      Log out of the streaming data mesh.
  version     Version of the CLI.
```

We will cover every command, but we will not cover every subcommand. For those subcommands not covered, the description provided in the help pages will suffice.

The help information follows a pattern. Example 6-3 shows this to help you better understand it in this chapter.

Example 6-3. A self-service CLI that allows full workflow access

```
./cli/sdm.py the_command  --help
Usage: sdm.py the_command [OPTIONS] COMMAND [ARGS]... ❶

  This is where the description of the command appears. ❷

Options:❸
  --the_option  This is the description of the option.

Commands:❹
  sub-command1  This is the description of sub-command1 ❺
  sub-command2  This is the description of sub-command2
  sub-command3  This is the description of sub-command3
```

❶ This is how the command is written on the command line. [ARGS] are any additional arguments that should be provided to the command.

❷ The description of the current command.

❸ This lists any options that can be provided to the command. These are placed in the [OPTIONS] part of the Usage.

❹ Starts a list of subcommands.

❺ The subcommand and its description.

Resource-Related Commands

Resources are hardware, software, or infrastructure that needs to be provisioned for a domain. Examples of resources for a domain are a streaming platform like Kafka cluster, a stream processing platform (ksqlDB, SaaS streaming platform), a Kafka Connect cluster, the connectors that deploy into a connect cluster, and UDFs.

In the spirit of serverless, automation of self-services is very convenient, especially for some resources that will always be needed. For example, when provisioning a domain, the streaming platform, the stream processing platform, and the connect cluster would get provisioned automatically. Other resources (such as UDFs and connectors) are provided as needed by all domains.

In this section, we will use the CLI to experience how a domain would interact with the streaming data mesh by first logging in to it, then showing examples of how to provision resources.

Cluster-Related Commands

A *cluster* is a resource that represents the streaming platform(s) in a domain. The `cluster` command allows domain personas to interact with the streaming platforms. There can be more than one platform, so this command allows you to list and describe each streaming platform.

In Example 6-4, notice there are no commands that allow you to create or delete a cluster. This is optional. Provisioning clusters is expensive. The omission of create and delete commands requires the domain personas to plan and present their request to the central team for approval. The central team will provision the clusters for the domain, once approved.

Example 6-4. A self-service CLI that allows full workflow access

```
./cli/sdm.py cluster  --help
Usage: sdm.py cluster [OPTIONS] COMMAND [ARGS]...

  cluster tool

Options:
  --help  Show this message and exit.

Commands:
  describe  Describes a streaming platform.
```

```
    list      Lists all the streaming platform clusters
    topic     topic tool
```

Planning and presenting will require the reasons for the request to create or delete, and a future architecture diagram that stays within the streaming data mesh requirements for security and data governance.

Topic-Related Commands

Topics are resources that hold data in a streaming platform. Hence `topic` is a subcommand of `cluster`. These streaming platforms all provide CLIs that allow users to create topics with default values that follow best practices. Wrapping these CLIs with your own `smd.py` CLI will help simplify the command for the domain personas.

Example 6-5 shows a self-service CLI tool that is extremely easy for domain engineers to use.

Example 6-5. A self-service CLI that creates a topic

```
$ ./cli/sdm.py cluster topic create \
    --name foo \ ❶
    --cluster-id bar ❷
```

❶ The topic name

❷ The cluster ID to create the topic in

Example 6-6 shows additional commands available for topics.

Example 6-6. Creating and connecting to a cluster

```
$ ./cli/sdm.py cluster topic -h
Usage:
  streaming-data-mesh.sh cluster topic [command]

Available Commands:
  list         List all available topics in the Kafka cluster in your domain.
  create       Creates a topic
  delete       Delete a topic
  publish      Published the topic as a data product.
               This will generate an AsyncAPI and send it
               to the streaming data catalog.
  consume      Consume the data in the topic
  produce      Produce some data to the topic
  describe     Describes a topic

Flags:
  --name       Unique name of topic
```

The domain Commands

The domain commands of the CLI let you list and describe each domain. You can also request access to a data product from another domain (see Example 6-7).

Example 6-7. Requesting access to a streaming data product

```
./cli/sdm.py domain  --help
Usage: sdm.py domain [OPTIONS] COMMAND [ARGS]...

  domain command

Options:
  --help  Show this message and exit.

Commands:
  describe  Describes a domain including location, owners, and published...
  list      Lists all the domains in the data mesh
  request   Requests access to a data product by the current (your) domain.
```

Requesting access to a streaming data product will initiate a workflow that creates a replication process from the producing domain into the requesting domain's streaming platform (see Example 6-8). The workflow will be prefixed with the producing domain's ID to avoid topic name collisions. The workflow executed behind this command is as follows:

- Ensure that the producing domain's streaming platform has the capacity to serve a new domain. If not, a notification should be sent to the producing domain of the requirement to increase capacity.

- Ensure that the consuming domain's streaming platform has the capacity to consume a new streaming data product. If not, a notification should be sent to the consuming domain to increase capacity.

- Send a request for approval to the producing domain to consume the data. The producing domain then executes a grant command that starts the process of providing read-only access to the topic and provisioning a replication process between the two streaming platforms.

Example 6-8. Requesting access to a streaming data product

```
./cli/sdm.py domain request  --help
Usage: sdm.py domain request [OPTIONS] DOMAIN_ID DATA_PRODUCT_ID

  Requests access to a data product by the current (your) domain.

Arguments:
  DOMAIN_ID       [required]
  DATA_PRODUCT_ID  [required]
```

```
Options:
  --help  Show this message and exit.
```

The connect Commands

The connect commands, shown in Example 6-9, interact with the connect cluster. As you may recall, the connect cluster runs connectors that move data in and out of a streaming platform.

Example 6-9. The connect command context

```
./cli/sdm.py connect   --help
Usage: sdm.py connect [OPTIONS] COMMAND [ARGS]...

  connector tool

Options:
  --help  Show this message and exit.

Commands:
  connector  Tool to manage connectors
  describe   Describes a connect cluster
  list       Lists all the connect clusters
```

At first, the connect cluster will not have any connectors. In Example 6-10, the add command adds connectors to the connect cluster. It checks whether you have the connector libraries, and if not, it pulls them from a central repository that the central team manages. We will talk more about the role the central repository plays in Chapter 7.

Example 6-10. The connector command

```
./cli/sdm.py connect connector  --help
Usage: sdm.py connect connector [OPTIONS] COMMAND [ARGS]...

  Tool to manage connectors

Options:
  --help  Show this message and exit.

Commands:
  add       Retrieves a connector from the repository and configures it.
  deployed  Lists all the deployed connectors
  describe  Describes a connector, parameters
  drop      Drops a connector
  list      Available connectors from the repository to add
  restart   Restarts a connector
  start     Starts a connector
```

```
    stop      Stops a connector
    update    Updates a connector to a newer version
```

Example 6-11 shows you how to bring a connector into the connect cluster and configure it to run.

Example 6-11. Adding a connector

```
./cli/sdm.py connect connector add  --help
Usage: sdm.py connect connector add [OPTIONS] CONNECT_CLUSTER_ID
                                    [CONNECTOR_CONFIG]

  Retrieves a connector from the repository and  configures it. Returns a
  connector id

Arguments:
  CONNECT_CLUSTER_ID  [required]
  [CONNECTOR_CONFIG]  connector configuration file

Options:
  --help  Show this message and exit.
```

The streaming Commands

The streaming commands allow you to interact with the stream processing platform. To review, the stream processing platform runs SQL statements that transform data derivatives into streaming data products. Example 6-12 includes two important commands to know about: udf and sql.

Example 6-12. The streaming command

```
./cli/sdm.py streaming  --help
Usage: sdm.py streaming [OPTIONS] COMMAND [ARGS]...

  streaming context

Options:
  --help  Show this message and exit.

Commands:
  describe  Describes a streaming cluster
  sql       Tool to manage SQL statements
  udf       Tool to manage UDFs
```

The udf command

The udf command is very similar to the connect add command in that it searches the central repository for UDFs you want to add to your UDF library. To review, UDFs are user-defined functions that can be used in the SQL that transforms data to create streaming data products. Example 6-13 shows a list of commands that will allow you to manage UDFs.

Example 6-13. The udf command

```
./cli/sdm.py streaming udf --help
Usage: sdm.py streaming udf [OPTIONS] COMMAND [ARGS]...

  Tool to manage UDFs

Options:
  --help  Show this message and exit.

Commands:
  add       Add an available UDF
  describe  Describes a UDF, parameters, data types, return value
  drop      Drops a UDF
  list      Available UDFs from the repository to add
  update    Updates a UDF to a newer version
```

The central team will again use a central repository to manage all the artifacts (connectors and UDFs) needed for domains to build streaming data products.

The sql command

The `sql` command in the `streaming` context will allow you to manage the SQL statements used to transform data into streaming data products (see Example 6-14). Most stream processing platforms allow you to develop and deploy completely within their interfaces. We need to compose a set of tasks when deploying SQL statements for stream processing:

- Send a request to OpenLineage to insert or remove the SQL in the lineage graph of the streaming data product. The SQL will need to be parsed to identify the source and destination so that OpenLineage can join it with other SQL and connections processing the same data. This is what enables building the lineage graph piecewise.
- Assemble the source and destination schemas to attach to the OpenLineage graph.
- Identify the topics for the source and destinations.
- Deploy the SQL into the stream processing platform.

Example 6-14 lists some additional commands with their corresponding definitions. The commands add, drop, start, stop, restart, and update all need to interact with OpenLineage to make the necessary updates to ensure that it remains accurate.

Example 6-14. The `sql` context

```
./cli/sdm.py streaming sql --help
Usage: sdm.py streaming sql [OPTIONS] COMMAND [ARGS]...

  Tool to manage SQL statements

Options:
  --help  Show this message and exit.

Commands:
  add      Add a sql to the stream processing platform
  drop     Deletes a sql
  explain  Explains a sql
  list     List all available sql with status:running/stopped/error.
  ps       List all running sql with id.
  restart  Restarts a sql
  start    Starts a sql
  stop     Stops a sql
  update   Updates/replaces a deployed sql
```

Example 6-15 shows how to deploy a SQL statement into the stream processing platform. If the SQL cannot be parsed to identify the sources and destination, they can be provided optionally as arguments to this command. Parsing SQL can be difficult, especially if it's complex. Notice that the --sources option is plural. This is to support joining multiple streams together and outputting to another stream.

Example 6-15. Deploying a SQL statement to the stream processing platform

```
./cli/sdm.py streaming sql add --help
Usage: sdm.py streaming sql add [OPTIONS] SQLFILE DESCRIPTION

  Add a sql to the stream processing platform

Arguments:
  SQLFILE      [required]
  DESCRIPTION  [required]

Options:
  --sources TEXT
  --destination TEXT
  --help
```

Publishing a Streaming Data Product

When a streaming data product is ready to be published, the data will be in a topic in the streaming platform. As you may recall from previous chapters, publishing a streaming data product requires a lot of work.

The complexity of publishing a streaming data mesh is completely hidden from the domain personas (see Example 6-16). Only the topic, the cluster in which the topic resides, the name, and the description of the streaming data product are required. All the necessary information and tasks are assembled by the implementation of this self-service.

First, we need to assemble all the metadata associated with the data product. This includes the following:

- Name and description
- The schema that represents its format, maybe even an example
- The entire lineage graph, including streaming data products from other domains

Then we need to perform the following tasks:

- Constructing an AsyncAPI YAML document
- Registering the AsyncAPI YAML to the streaming data catalog
- Securing the topic with proper access controls
- Adding monitoring agents

Some businesses may want to add more to this list. At a minimum, these tasks should be executed. As Example 6-16 shows, an entire workflow should be built to diagram the steps of publishing a streaming data product (more on this in Chapter 7).

Example 6-16. Publishing a streaming data product

```
./cli/sdm.py cluster topic publish  --help
Usage: sdm.py cluster topic publish [OPTIONS] CLUSTER_ID TOPIC NAME
                                    DESCRIPTION

  Publishes a topic as a streaming data product

Arguments:
  CLUSTER_ID   [required]
  TOPIC        [required]
  NAME         [required]
  DESCRIPTION  [required]

Options:
  --help  Show this message and exit.
```

Data Governance-Related Services

Data governance-related services are also domain-facing services. They allow domains to work together in a mesh by enforcing policies that enable interoperability and trustability. Every business will have its own self-defined data governance policies. These policies get translated to services in the streaming data mesh.

Data governance services are divided into three categories:

Security services
> Relates to authorizing and authenticating consuming domains and the contents of the streaming data product

Standards services
> Relates to enforcement of standard patterns like addresses, phone numbers, etc.

Lineage services
> Relates to capturing cross-domain lineage paths for streaming data products

We will talk about data governance-related services at a high level. Many details of this section (especially security) can get too deep and disrupt the goal of this book, which is to design a streaming data mesh. We will annotate topics in this section if they start to digress from our goal.

Security Services

When domain engineers build streaming data products, they need a set of security-related services to secure them. These security services can be broken into three distinct groups: data obfuscation, identity, and auditing.

Data obfuscation services

Data obfuscation is the process of obscuring sensitive data from hackers or bad actors. By obscuring the data, these bad actors will not be able to retrieve the original data. We can obfuscate data in two ways: encryption and tokenization.

Encryption. *Encryption* is the process of obscuring data using an encryption method. It involves providing a security key to the consuming domain so it can decrypt the data. Only consuming domains with the key would have the ability to do this. The assumption is that bad actors would be less likely to obtain the key to decrypt sensitive data. Two services aid in this process:

- Key management service (KMS)
- A tool (in our case, the CLI) that will interface with the KMS

Security keys are provided by a KMS that generates public and private key pairs needed for transferring encrypted data. All the major cloud providers have a built-in KMS. Public keys are used to encrypt the data, and the private keys are used to decrypt the data. The domain producers use the public keys to encrypt sensitive data, while the private keys are held by the consuming domain.

The public and private key pairs are created by the consuming domain. The private keys are held by the consuming domain, and the public keys are sent to the producing domain to encrypt data.

Alternatively the producing domain could create the public and private key pairs (or just *key pairs*) and send the private keys to the consuming domains. This breaks public/private key best practices. Details of encryption are beyond of the scope of this book.

Along with key exchanges, the KMS also performs a set of management tasks for the keys generated for all domains. For example, the KMS provides key pair information for existing domains for regulatory audits. Another task is to execute key rotations to minimize key exposure in case the keys are compromised.

Using the CLI, key exchanges can be done easily between domains while being tracked and monitored by the KMS. Example 6-17 is a possible command-line tool that can do this key exchange. The implementation would require a workflow that handles the specific tasks the business requires, like approvals, notifications, and correlating key pairs between data products and domains.

Example 6-17. Possible tool for granting access to a streaming data product that includes generating public and private keys

```
./cli/sdm.py dp access grant --help
Usage: sdm.py dp access grant [OPTIONS] DATA_PRODUCT_ID CONSUMING_DOMAIN

  Grants access to a data product to a consuming domain.

Arguments:
  DATA_PRODUCT_ID   [required] ❶
  CONSUMING_DOMAIN  [required] ❷

Options:
  --remove / --no-remove  [default: no-remove]
  --help
```

❶ DATA_PRODUCT_ID identifies the streaming data product to encrypt with the public key.

❷ CONSUMING_DOMAIN sends the public key to the producing domain to encrypt data. It sends a record of this interaction to the KMS for regulatory inquiries.

Encryption and decryption UDFs. A UDF that performs encryption would be used by the domain producing the streaming data product. For example, in ksqlDB, you want to use a UDF to encrypt fields that have sensitive data. This UDF should already be part of a workflow that provisions infrastructure. Examples 6-18 and 6-19 show how these UDFs could be used to encrypt and decrypt data, respectively. Example 6-20 shows how to get a list of UDFs.

Example 6-18. UDF that encrypts sensitive data

```
insert into data_product_encrypted
    first_name,
    last_name,
    encrypt(SSN, `public_key`) ❶
from data_product_raw
```

❶   encrypt() is a UDF that encrypts the SSN, given a public key.

Example 6-19. UDF that decrypts sensitive data

```
insert into data_product_decrypted
    first_name,
    last_name,
    dencrypt(SSN, `private_key`) ❶
from data_product_encrypted
```

❶   decrypt() is a UDF that decrypts the SSN, given a private key.

Example 6-20. Get a list of UDFs

```
$ ./cli/sdm.py streaming udf list ❶
```

❶   This gets a list of UDFs for domain engineers to use when writing SQL.

Tokenization and detokenization UDFs. Tokenization, as you may recall, is a different approach to obfuscating data. This approach requires the consuming domain to look up the original value from a tokenization system. Think of a tokenization system as a database for tokens where you can easily and quickly look up a token and be returned its original value.

Tokenized data cannot be decrypted and does not require key pairs. The only necessary requirements are two UDFs, one that takes the original value and returns the token, and another that takes a token and returns the original value (see Examples 6-21 and 6-22).

Example 6-21. UDF that tokenizes sensitive data

```
insert into data_product_tokenized
    first_name,
    last_name,
    toke(SSN) ❶
from data_product_raw
```

❶ toke() is a UDF that takes the SSN and returns a token that can be used as a key to look up the original SSN value.

Example 6-22. UDF that de-tokenizes sensitive data

```
insert into data_product_detokenized
    first_name,
    last_name,
    detoke(SSN) ❶
from data_product_tokenized
```

❶ detoke() is a UDF that uses the token to look up the original SSN value.

Sensitive information detection. Many businesses have started projects to build services that can detect data containing sensitive content. These services are implemented as machine learning models embedded within the data pipeline that generates the streaming data product. Being able to detect sensitive data definitely isn't a requirement for a streaming data mesh. But it is a very convenient feature to have when you do not know whether you have sensitive data.

For example, a comment field in your data where users can put any descriptive information could be dangerous. Being able to detect any comments including sensitive data like SSNs would help domain engineers understand their data better and know when to obfuscate their data or at least omit it from the data product.

Identity services

Identity services provide authorization and authentication for domains and their streaming data products. Many times, the infrastructure provisioned for a domain already has a way to integrate with identity services. For example, Kafka has a few ways to authenticate and authorize the consuming domain's access to topics, one of which is to look up users or roles from an identity service.

As mentioned in the previous section, key pairs allow domain consumers to encrypt and decrypt the streaming data product. This same approach can also be used to identify domains and provide their access to the streaming data product. Mutual Transport Layer Security (mTLS) is a standard protocol that provides authentication (or access) and encryption between two systems (or domains).

The CLI tool can completely hide the encryption, authorization, and authentication implementations from the domains to simplify the experience of sharing data between domains in a streaming data mesh. Other methods of authorization include:

Kerboros
> This security mechanism provides identity information so domains can identify each other and provide access controls. Paired with plain TLS (without the "m"), encryption can be implemented.

Key/secret mechanism
> This mechanism provides a simpler way domains can provide access to each other's data products. The key/secret will be mapped to the actual identities so that domain product owners can clearly identify them. This mechanism usually requires manual rotation to protect from compromised keys/secrets. Also paired with TLS, this method enables both identity and encryption.

Open Authentication (OAuth)
> This is an open standard allows access between applications, or in our case, domains.

Streaming platforms act as "ports." We talked about ports in Chapter 3. Ports represent the input and output connections to and from domains in a streaming data mesh. They make up the "mesh" in a streaming data mesh.

In earlier chapters, we mentioned that data products pass through input and output ports. Producers write data products through output ports, and consumers read data products through input ports. These ports need to be secured using the identity services and authorization mechanism chosen by the business. This process is complex. Since domains authorize access to streaming data products, they need simple-to-use self-services that make this complex authorization process easy. The complexity is hidden from the domain personas.

Example 6-23 presents more commands that provide information on the data products that have been granted access to a domain. The describe command lists all the domains currently with access to a given streaming data product, and possible usage metrics.

Example 6-23. A self-service tool that can grant access to a streaming data product for a domain

```
./cli/sdm.py dp access  --help
Usage: sdm.py dp access [OPTIONS] COMMAND [ARGS]...

  access controls for data products

Options:
  --help  Show this message and exit.
```

```
Commands:
  describe  Describes an access control list including the data product...
  grant     Grants access to a data product to a consuming domain.
  list      List all access controls including all the data products and...
```

Auditing

Audit logging is the practice of capturing security changes, such as when a domain is granted access to a streaming data product. These changes get written to a logging service so that security auditors can monitor it. If any suspicious activities are occurring, actions can be taken to head off the potential threat. Audit logging has two parts: the logging activity itself and a way to query the activity.

Audit logging should be built into the domain's infrastructure without domain engineering knowledge. For example, in Example 6-23 in the previous section, granting access to a data product will also log the act of granting into the audit log. It should instead be built into the granting workflow. In Chapter 7, we will talk more about workflows behind the self-services in a streaming data mesh.

Data product owners also need to know the existence of this audit log and possibly query it. If granting access to a streaming data product fails, or to generate reports for regulatory purposes, this audit log is extremely helpful.

This audit logging service may just be a web application that allows data product owners to query activity. It's critical for data product owners to keep track of the domains accessing their data products, especially when revoking access is necessary, such as when there is inactivity or when a data product has reached its end of life.

Standards Services

Services related to standards help provide tools to maintain interoperability between domains. In Chapter 4, we used a stream processing engine like ksqlDB or a SaaS stream processor to transform data so that it meets high-quality standards. The rules for these standards are defined by the federated data governance, as discussed in Chapter 5, but are enforced by the standards services.

One such tool that provides these services is a schema registry. A few open source tools provide a schema registry for free: Karapace and Apicurio. Many of these schema registries also support multiple data serialization types, like Avro, protobuf, and JSON. Schema registries provide the following capabilities:

Schema registration
> Schema registries allow producing domains to register their schemas assigned to a streaming data product so that consuming domains can retrieve them. This allows for consuming domains to understand how to read or parse the data product and relate to their use cases.

Schema validation

> Some streaming platforms are able to use the schema registry to validate incoming data to ensure that it conforms to its assigned schema. Schema validation protects consumers from invalid data that could take down their applications. Data product consumers use a schema registry to understand how to read the data. If the data doesn't conform to the schema, the consumer will fail.

Schema evolution

> applications in a producing domain will always be evolving. It's a sign of increased usage and potentially higher revenue. The evolution process, however, needs to follow federated data governance rules that include schemas. The schema registries have features that can enforce compatibilities between different versions of the schema. Here are some compatibility rules that the schema registry could enforce:
>
> *Backward*
>> This rule allows for deletion of fields and addition of optional fields.
>
> *Forward*
>> This rule allows for addition of new required fields and deletion of optional fields.
>
> *Full*
>> This rule allows for the addition and deletion of optional fields only.
>
> *None*
>> This rule allows for any changes to occur to the schema. This option is not recommended.

As you may recall in Chapter 5, the initial definition of a schema is owned by the producing domain. But the evolution of that schema is owned by the federated data governance and enforced by the schema registry. You will need to validate the new version of your schema against the schema registry to ensure that it is compliant. This should be part of the development lifecycle of the streaming data product.

Validation rules

> The Avro data serialization type provides a way to define *logical types* that extend existing Avro types like `string`, `long`, `boolean`, etc., and some complex types. This enables domains to provide validation rules to the fields of the data product. These rules help streaming data products conform to the standards defined by the federated data governance. Example 6-24 shows validation rules for a phone number.

Example 6-24. Avro schema that provides validation rules for a phone number

```
{
    "type": "record",
    "name": "myrecord",
    "fields": [
        {
            "name": "number",
            "doc": "Phone number inside the national network. Length
                between 4-14",
            "type": {
                "type": "string",
                "logicalType": "validatedString",
                "pattern":
                "^(\+\d{1,2}\s)?\(?\d{3}\)?[\s.-]\d{3}[\s.-]\d{4}$" ❶
            }
        }
    ]
}
```

❶ `pattern` provides a regular expression (RegEx) that validates a phone number.

The regular expression provided in the `pattern` field provides the validation rules for any phone number in the following formats:

```
123-456-7890
(123) 456-7890
123 456 7890
123.456.7890
+91 (123) 456-7890
```

Some existing schema validation tools can test your data to see if it conforms to the schema. These tools may need to be extended to allow for custom types, like the phone number type in Example 6-24. These validation tools can be embedded in the development process through unit tests that check for both valid and invalid formats. These validation tools and development practices will contribute to the overall health of the streaming data mesh.

Lineage Services

In Chapter 5 we talked about using a tool like OpenLineage to keep track of all the steps a streaming data product goes through in a single place. OpenLineage provides a set of services that allows domain engineers to send information about how data is being processed. It then is able to construct a lineage graph that can span multiple domains.

Examples 6-25 and 6-26 are `curl` requests to OpenLineage indicating that a process has started and completed. OpenLineage builds a graph of all these calls that reference the same job and inputs. The end result is a lineage graph.

Example 6-25. A `curl` request to OpenLineage to indicate that a job or a task has started

```
$ curl -X POST http://localhost:5000/api/v1/lineage \
  -H 'Content-Type: application/json' \
  -d '{
       "eventType": "START",
       "eventTime": "2020-12-28T19:52:00.001+10:00",
       "run": {
         "runId": "d46e465b-d358-4d32-83d4-df660ff614dd"
       },
       "job": { ❶
         "namespace": "my-namespace",
         "name": "my-job"
       },
       "inputs": [{ ❷
         "namespace": "my-namespace",
         "name": "my-input"
       }],
       "producer": "https://github.com/OpenLineage/OpenLineage/blob/v1-0-0/client"
     }'
```

❶ job shows information about the job or process that was performed on the data.

❷ input shows information about the data that was processed.

Example 6-26. A `curl` request to OpenLineage to indicate that a job or a task has completed

```
$ curl -X POST http://localhost:5000/api/v1/lineage \
  -H 'Content-Type: application/json' \
  -d '{
       "eventType": "COMPLETE",
       "eventTime": "2020-12-28T20:52:00.001+10:00",
       "run": {
         "runId": "d46e465b-d358-4d32-83d4-df660ff614dd"
       },
       "job": { ❶
         "namespace": "my-namespace",
         "name": "my-job"
       },
       "outputs": [{ ❷
         "namespace": "my-namespace",
         "name": "my-output",
         "facets": {
```

```
      "schema": {  ❸
        "_producer": "https://github.com/OpenLineage/OpenLineage/blob
                      /v1-0-0/client",
        "_schemaURL": "https://github.com/OpenLineage/OpenLineage/blob
                      /v1-0-0/spec/OpenLineage.json#/definitions
                      /SchemaDatasetFacet",
        "fields": [
          { "name": "a", "type": "VARCHAR"},
          { "name": "b", "type": "VARCHAR"}
        ]
      }
    }
  }],
  "producer": "https://github.com/OpenLineage/OpenLineage/blob/v1-0-0/client"
}'
```

❶ job shows information about the job or process that was performed on the data.

❷ output shows information about the output of the process so that OpenLineage can link it with other jobs .

❸ schema shows information about how the data looks after it was processed.

All of these data governance services do not require any coding and very little configuration. They are provisioned and maintained by the central team, so domains do not need the skill set to do so.

Many of these data governance services are already provided by SaaS providers. Using a SaaS provider will simplify much of this work and minimize the responsibilities of the central team.

SaaS Services and APIs

Cloud SaaS services allow you to relinquish almost all the responsibilities of managing the infrastructure you need for your streaming data mesh. They also provide all the tools to interact with the infrastructure so that you can easily perform all the resource- and data governance-related tasks that are part of the streaming data mesh. This includes the KMS work previously discussed.

The work still required for you is to aggregate these tools and services that are fully managed in the cloud to self-service services that are easy to use by domains. The self-services need to be backed by workflows that satisfy business needs and data governance requirements.

You can use various tools to make it simple to provision infrastructure in the cloud. They all have a way to be integrated into build processes or workflows. The advantage these tools have are repeatability and consistency when provisioning, which saves time and frustration. Here are some tools to consider:

- Terraform
- Ansible
- Chef
- Puppet

Each of the major cloud providers also provides CLIs that can be integrated into integration processes or workflows. These can do the same work as the tools just mentioned.

Summary

The streaming data mesh CLI in this chapter provides a simple model for domains to interact with the data mesh. It forces domains to follow a workflow to build data products while ensuring that all governance requirements are met. This model can be extended or customized for the specific needs of the business. In Chapter 7, these workflows will be important as architect a streaming data mesh.

Architecting a Streaming Data Mesh

In Chapters 3 through 6, we covered the pillars of a streaming data mesh. Now we will use that knowledge to architect a streaming data mesh. As we mentioned earlier in this book, the term "mesh" in "data mesh" was taken from the term "service mesh" in microservice architectures. We build upon that similarity to describe the parts of a streaming data mesh by using the same terms used to describe parts of a microservice architecture. We will describe each part of the architecture, so knowledge of microservice architecture is not a prerequisite. We will also consider multiple streaming data mesh solutions and list their benefits and trade-offs. The outcome will be an easy and clear framework that can be used to implement your own streaming data mesh.

Infrastructure

As stated in Chapter 1, we will be implementing a streaming data mesh with Kafka. Using Kafka is optional and can be replaced with Apache Pulsar or Redpanda; whichever you choose, we recommend using a fully managed and serverless streaming platform to relinquish the tasks of self-managing infrastructure. Likewise we will use ksqlDB as the stream processing engine. It is also available as a fully-managed or self-managed service. The following are some options that are fully managed:

- DeltaStream
- Popsink
- Decodable
- Materialized
- RisingWave
- Timeplus

Both Kafka and ksqlDB are stream processing engines that use SQL as the primary way of building streaming data pipelines. There may be others, but at the time of writing this book, these two options stand out the most.

We talked about the self-services and related workflows needed to support the domains in Chapter 6. These same self-services and workflows will work whether you use a fully managed service or are self-managing your infrastructure. Later in this chapter we will provide ideas on how to implement these self-services as workflows.

Two Architecture Solutions

We have two options when designing a streaming data mesh—a dedicated streaming infrastructure within the domains, or a shared, multitenant infrastructure in which each domain is a tenant (see Figures 7-1 and 7-2).

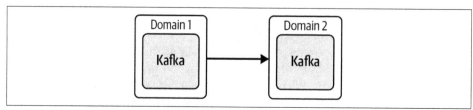

Figure 7-1. Dedicated infrastructure

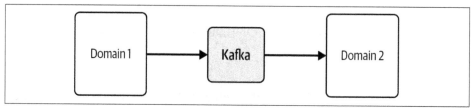

Figure 7-2. Multitenant infrastructure

Both diagrams include the streaming platform (Kafka, Pulsar, Redpanda). What is not visible are the stream processing platform (ksqlDB, SaaS stream processor) and the Kafka Connect cluster because their existence is implied. The only difference between the two diagrams is the location of the streaming platform. To summarize the purpose of each, the *streaming platform* is the messaging system that streams data (or events) and holds them inside topics. The *stream processing platform* is the system that transforms (enrichment and cleansing) data between topics in the streaming platform. Lastly, the connect cluster holds connectors that integrate systems (like databases) with the streaming platform to get its data into or out of a topic.

In both options, producers and consumers (or the clients) of streaming data products produce and consume locally. This means that the clients are accessing infrastructure that was provisioned near or preferably in the same global region. This is a rule that should be followed to maintain a good experience in a streaming data mesh. If the infrastructure isn't close, these clients will have to communicate with their infrastructure over long distances, creating lag and other ill effects in their applications.

If there are long distances to deal with, use a replication mechanism to bring the data locally to the clients. Replication is the process of moving data between streaming platforms like Kafka. It's a process that is hidden from clients consuming or producing to Kafka. The clients, therefore, are not exposed to the unforeseen effects that long distances can create for them. Let's now discuss the two options in more detail.

Dedicated Infrastructure

This option deploys the infrastructure—streaming platform, stream processing platform, and Kafka Connect—into the domains so that the only user (tenant) that can use them is the domain itself; hence they are dedicated infrastructure to the domains.

This option comes with some advantages:

- Security implementation is easier because there are no other domains (tenants) to separate in the infrastructure. This reduces the number of self-services the central engineers need to develop and makes it easier to manage. This reduction of complexity could translate to the reduction of security risks.
- The infrastructure is provisioned in the same region as the domain. This keeps all the data derivatives local, which increases performance of the infrastructure components. It also reduces cost of cross-region data movement in the cloud. Cross-region data movement is limited to the replication of streaming data products to other domains.
- Usage metrics are easier to relate to domains. Logs are already separated and can be associated to specific consumers for easy billing for charge-backs. This includes the audit logs for easier monitoring of security access in the domains.
- Scalability can be applied specifically to domains without affecting other domains. Scaling infrastructure up or down can be disruptive. Limiting disruption to a specific domain will make a better experience for all unaffected domains.
- If a domain guarantees uptime SLAs to a consumer, a DR plan can be implemented specifically to the domain/data product that meets those guarantees.

The only disadvantage is the cost of provisioning infrastructure to all the domains. This could be lowered with the use of SaaS providers that fully manage this infrastructure.

There are two types of domains: a domain that produces streaming data products and a domain that consumes streaming data products. A domain can also be both. Since the infrastructure is dedicated to the domains, we will describe how the infrastructure will be deployed in them.

Producing domain architecture

A *producing domain* is a domain that only produces data products. It does not consume data products from other domains. In Figure 7-3, a Kafka cluster, Connect cluster, and a ksqlDB cluster are provisioned.

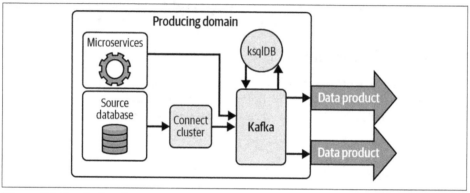

Figure 7-3. Producing domain

For dedicated infrastructure, this is the minimum a domain needs. The Connect cluster reads data from the operational (source) database and feeds it to Kafka. The cleansing, transformation, and obfuscation of the data derivative is done in ksqlDB before it is fed to a final Kafka topic to be published as a streaming data product.

If your source comes only from microservices, there is reason not to have a Connect cluster. Likewise, if your data doesn't need any transformation or cleansing, you can omit the ksqlDB cluster. Most likely, a domain will need both a Connect cluster and a stream processing cluster to build streaming data products.

High-throughput producing domain

For domains that provide higher-throughput streaming data products, we recommend splitting the Kafka cluster to a write and read cluster (see Figure 7-4). This allows each cluster to scale separately. The write cluster is optimized for handling the high-throughput writes. The read cluster focuses on serving the streaming data products to its consumers with specific SLA guarantees. The replication between the write and read clusters can be handled by Kafka connectors or *cluster linking*—a proprietary technology provided by Confluent that makes data replication easy. It relieves the burden of having to manage more components by the central team.

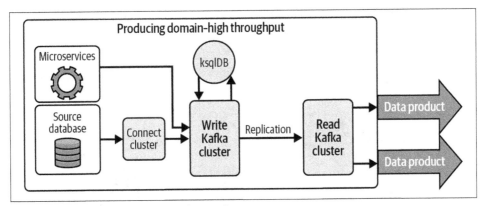

Figure 7-4. High-throughput producing domain

Likewise, this pattern works if the read cluster is intended to serve many consumers, which increases the read throughput. In this case, the write cluster could be scaled lower than the read cluster.

Having two Kafka clusters provides a way for failover in cases of disaster. This also increases resiliency. Each cluster can fail over to the other. This would require the two clusters to have same capacity. The failover coordination is something the central team will need to handle automatically. Failover is not a skill set domains need to know. Details of disaster recovery are outside the scope of this book.

Consuming domain architecture

Figure 7-5 illustrates how data from the producing domain gets replicated into the Kafka cluster in the consuming domain. To be clear, there is a Kafka cluster in the producing domain and the consuming domain. Streaming data is replicated from the Kafka in the producing domain to the Kafka in the consuming domain. How this replication is done will be discussed in "Data Plane" on page 142. The important thing to know here is that the application performing the replication lives in the consuming domain. If the producing domain has implemented a charge-back approach, the consuming workload will not be part of that cost because it's in the consuming domain's infrastructure.

Use this architecture if you want to maintain a Kappa architecture within the consuming domain. The data remains a stream and allows further processing using ksqlDB without landing in a database first.

This architecture enables the consuming domain to produce streaming data products too. It has the same infrastructure as the producing domain. In Chapter 2 we mentioned that an advantage of a streaming data mesh is streaming support for both real-time use cases and batch. We also warned of the costly technical debt to pay if a batch-only domain suddenly needs real-time use cases without the supporting infrastructure. Having a Kafka cluster in the consuming domain protects you from that debt.

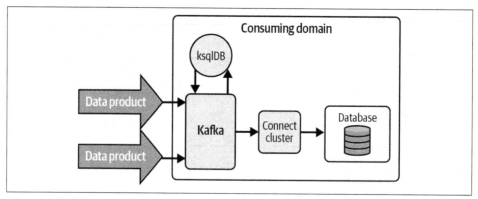

Figure 7-5. Consuming domain with Kafka, ksqlDB, and Connect cluster

Real-time online analytical processing databases. This architecture also provides integration with real-time online analytical processing (real-time OLAP, or RTOLAP) databases. RTOLAP databases can quickly retrieve, aggregate, and analyze data without having to run heavy batch processing. Figure 7-6 shows native integration with RTOLAP databases and omits the Connect cluster shown in Figure 7-5. Figure 7-6 shows a sample of the RTOLAP databases available in the market today: Rockset, Apache Pinot, Apache Druid, Materialized, Tinybird, and ClickHouse.

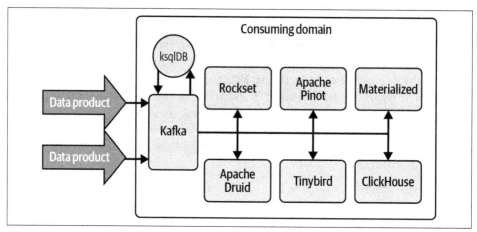

Figure 7-6. Integration with real-time OLAP databases

These RTOLAP databases can then serve data to real-time dashboards and applications at scale. With the streaming data mesh, you can maintain a Kappa architecture from the source in the producing domain to the real-time application in the consuming domain.

Consuming domains without a streaming platform. To reduce costs, it is optional to have only a Connect cluster provisioned in the consuming domain (see Figure 7-7). This option consumes data from the Kafka cluster in the producing domain and persists it in a database in the consuming domain.

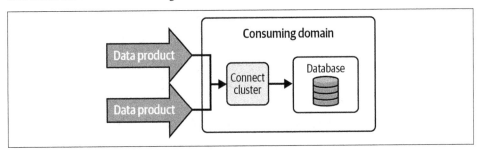

Figure 7-7. Connect cluster only in the consuming domain

This option prevents the domain from serving streaming data products itself. It also forces the domain to run batch processes to transform the data in the destination database. The transformation will be embedded in the data pipeline but will not be supported by the central team. This is because the destination database is outside the scope of the infrastructure provisioned by the central team.

Any batch processes embedded in the data pipeline will negate real-time capabilities in the domain. Changing this requires provisioning of a Kafka cluster and a ksqlDB cluster. Much effort will be required to reconfigure all the infrastructure to work like Figure 7-5. This is the technical debt we alluded to in Chapter 2.

This architecture also adds work to the central engineering team. They will have to support two methods of consuming streaming data products: replication between Kafka clusters (Figure 7-5) and connector-based consumption (Figure 7-7). Each method has its own workflow and self-services to build out the infrastructure. This option starts to become more of an antipattern that doesn't conform to the spirit of a streaming mesh.

Recommended architectures

Figure 7-8 illustrates of our recommended architecture for a streaming data mesh, because streaming data products appear locally to the consuming domains. You can compare this experience to shortcuts in the filesystem of your computer. Users can read and process the contents of the shortcut locally, which in actuality originate from a remote computer. In our case, the topics containing streaming data products in the consuming domain's Kafka cluster appear as if they are shortcuts that originate from the producing domain. Consumers read data locally, and the complexity of replicating the streaming data product is hidden.

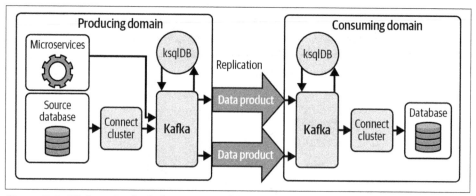

Figure 7-8. All domains look the same, enabling production and consumption of streaming data products

This architecture is also recommended because it makes provisioning infrastructure for the domains simple, making it less burdensome for the central team. All domains get provisioned with the same infrastructure: Kafka, ksqlDB, and Connect cluster. This allows any domain to produce and consume streaming data products.

Similarly, Figure 7-9 is an example of how to include RTOLAP databases for real-time data analytics. The RTOLAP databases can consume streaming data products directly from Kafka. ksqlDB also provides the capability to transform the streaming data product to a format that is easily consumable for RTOLAP databases. RTOLAP databases like their data preprocessed to reduce their workloads and focus on faster query execution.

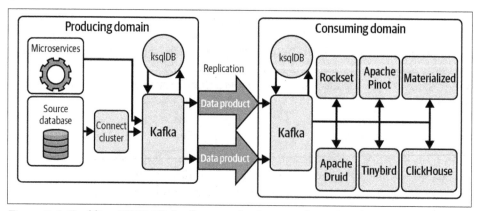

Figure 7-9. Enabling RTOLAP databases to further transform data by the consuming domain

Dedicated infrastructure makes managing a streaming data mesh a lot easier by its single-tenant approach. Security is made simple by this, as well as provisioning the infrastructure. Domains also don't experience "noisy neighbors" that are a result of other tenants using up resources. Scalability is simpler, making the domain's infrastructure elastic. However, all this can make the cost of a streaming data mesh very expensive. An alternative approach is to use a multitenant infrastructure for streaming data mesh.

Multitenant Infrastructure

In a *multitenant infrastructure*, Kafka is shared to multiple domains. Access controls are set to separate and protect domains from accessing sensitive data. This can reduce costs but increase complexity to the streaming data mesh.

In Figure 7-10, the Connect cluster is still provisioned inside the domain. ksqlDB is deployed only in the producing domain, which we'll address later in this section. Each domain also gets allocated part of the multitenant Kafka cluster using access controls.

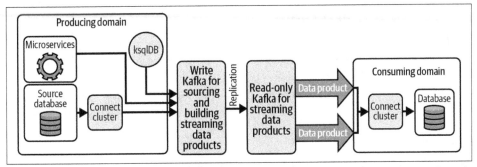

Figure 7-10. In this multitenant infrastructure, Kafka read and write clusters are shared across multiple domains

Since both Kafka clusters will be serving multiple producing and consuming domains, we again suggest separating the write clusters from the read clusters in order to be able to separately scale and ease management. This isolates the transformation workload for the streaming data products to only the write cluster. In Table 7-1 you can see a list of advantages for implementing this separation.

Table 7-1. Use cases for separating write and read Kafka clusters

Use case	Advantage
The number of consuming domains for the same streaming data product increases.	The read Kafka cluster can separately scale from the write. Increasing scalability requires rebalancing in Kafka so that the data maintains balanced data distribution, which in turn enables balanced data processing. The write cluster maintains its capacity and is unaffected by the change.
The data product has resource-intensive transformations.	The read Kafka cluster is unaffected by the transformation occurring in the write Kafka cluster and continues to serve streaming data products to consuming domains.
The write Kafka cluster goes down.	If the write Kafka goes down, the read cluster is unaffected and continues to serve consumers.

Producing domain architecture

In Figure 7-10 the producing domains look similar to the dedicated infrastructure discussed earlier in this chapter, except Kafka is a multitenant cluster and located in the central space. The write cluster will be used for streaming data product development. The Connect cluster in the domain will send source data derivatives to topics in the write cluster. ksqlDB will access those topics to transform the derivatives to build streaming data products. The final streaming data products are replicated from the write to the read Kafka cluster.

Streaming data products are replicated to the read cluster as part of publishing it. The separate read and write clusters help in isolating resources for development of streaming data products from resources that serve them. Again, the separation of read and write streaming platforms makes scaling easy without disruption from either.

Consuming domain architecture

The consuming domain in Figure 7-10 shows no ksqlDB, which takes away the ability to transform data in real time. If this consuming domain needs to further transform the data, these are alternatives:

- The consuming domain could use entirely different infrastructure outside of the streaming data mesh that it will have to self-manage. The Connect cluster in the consuming domain will most likely write to a data store, which immediately forces batching semantics. Persisting a streaming data product in a data store changes it to a batching data product.

- Use Apache Spark or Apache Flink to read the streaming data product right off the streaming platform. This will maintain streaming but requires deep skill sets in those technologies. Also, the infrastructure would be outside the scope of the central team's responsibility. This will take a consuming domain back to the monolithic-style data warehouses or lakes.

- Have the original producing domain create a new streaming data product that meets the consuming domain's requirements. This will not require the consuming domain to make further transformations.

Although some of these alternatives follow batching semantics, the data products are still streaming into the consuming domain, which still qualifies this solution to be a streaming data mesh. A streaming data mesh ensures that the data products are streaming from their origins to their consumers. How consumers ultimately use the streaming data products (batching or streaming) after they have been consumed is outside the requirements of a streaming data mesh.

It is important to know that without a stream processing platform like ksqlDB or a SaaS stream processor, domains cannot transform their data in real time. Data product transformations will need to be done in a database or in the source system itself. This starts to lean toward batching semantics. Even if Kafka Connect reads the database after the data products have been transformed, the resulting streaming data product will not truly be real-time but instead will be snapshots of the data product. Consumers will need to know this information so they can implement their use case expecting this behavior.

Regions

Most likely, your business will span more than one global region. If this is the case, it's important to keep the data local to the clients consuming it. As we've mentioned before, making clients reach across regions to produce or consume data will cause ill effects in the applications.

The solution is to reproduce the read-write streaming platform's model in each region and replicate that data asynchronously between regions. Figure 7-11 shows multiple global regions: Americas, EMEA, and APAC. The dotted lines represent asynchronous replication of data between the regions, and the solid lines represent clients producing and consuming data locally within those regions. The replication process is a streaming process, so real time is not lost.

It's important in this model to provide prefixes (or namespaces) to all the resources to avoid name collision within the streaming platforms. This includes topic names and schema names.

In Figure 7-12 let's say that the streaming data products flowing through the streaming data mesh contain employee information from different global regions. These domains were separated because all have different systems for payroll and benefits, and follow different regional regulations. Following the data governance rules in the streaming data mesh, it should be agreed upon that all these regions would conform to a single employee schema. This would prevent multiple redundant transformations in each region.

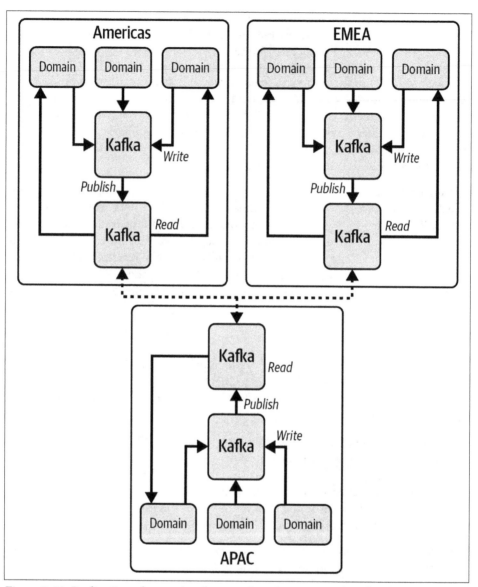

Figure 7-11. Replication of streaming data products between read Kafka clusters in each region

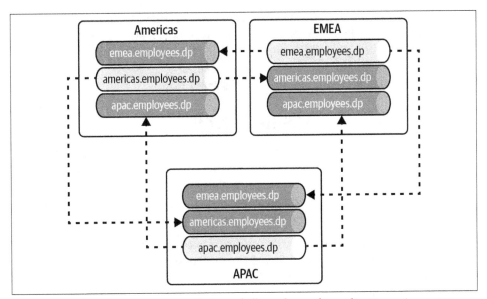

Figure 7-12. Creating an aggregated view of all employees by replication using name-spaced topics

The lightly shaded tubes in Figure 7-12 represent writable topics containing streaming data products that are written to locally. The other tubes represent read-only topics containing replicated data originating from the remote writable topic. This provides each region with a local topic from which to read streaming data products as well as a local writable topic that only the local region can write to.

To create a single global view of all the employees in the business, you would consume all three topics at the same time (see Example 7-1). Every region can create a global view of all employees merged into a single stream.

Example 7-1. Consuming multiple topics with the same suffix

```
consumer.subscribe(["*.employees.dp"])
```

This pattern would be the same for the dedicated infrastructure solution as well.

The dedicated and multitenant infrastructures are not mutually exclusive. We can have a mix of both. It does require more management and organization of infrastructure and metadata for the central team to handle. For example, it would be possible to allow dedicated infrastructure for the domains in the Americas, and limit the APAC and EMEA regions to multitenant infrastructure. In the cloud, those regions tend to be more expensive to provision infrastructure, and implementing a multitenancy in those regions might be a more cost-effective solution.

The two architectural solutions we've presented are for domains and how they share data with each other. They enable the domains to produce and consume streaming data products. There is a central component to the streaming data mesh that orchestrates and manages it and its domains that the central team is part of. It also has an architecture that is the heart of the streaming data mesh.

Streaming Data Mesh Central Architecture

The *central architecture* is everything outside of the domains. It's operated by the central team and manages all the self-services invoked by the CLI we introduced in Chapter 6. It also manages OpenLineage, Schema Registry, streaming data catalog, and others. In this section, we will list all the systems in the central architecture and see how the domains and the streaming data mesh intercommunicate.

Microservices have components called the data plane, control plane, and sidecar. Putting these components together forms a service mesh from which the term "mesh" was derived. The idea of a data mesh came from this architecture. We can map these components with our components in a streaming data mesh:

- The sidecar is the agents deployed within the domains that communicate with the control plane.
- The replication of data between domains is the data plane.
- The central streaming data mesh is the control plane (everything except the domains).

In this section, we will go over these mappings in detail. The term *data plane* will represent the replication of streaming data products between the domains and is controlled by the domain agents. We also will start calling the central streaming data mesh the *control plane*.

The Domain Agent (aka Sidecar)

In microservices, a sidecar is a component deployed with the microservice that communicates with a *control plane*. The control plane communicates with the sidecar to control the behavior of the microservices, configure their security, capture usage metrics, and configure the movement of data. This same idea can be used in a streaming data mesh.

This agent's sole purpose is to simply aggregate all the interactions between the domain and the streaming data mesh into a single component that can be easily deployed when provisioning the domain. The domain-facing CLI we talked about in Chapter 6 communicates with the control plane. The control plane then sends commands to the domain agent on behalf of the CLI as part of a command workflow. The following is a nonexhaustive list of command examples:

- Downloading and installing connectors and UDFs to their corresponding systems. The self-service hosted in the control plane will orchestrate a set of tasks that includes (1) searching for connectors or UDFs (the artifact) in a central repository, (2) commanding the domain agent to download the artifact locally to the domain, and then (3) instructing the domain to install or upgrade the existing artifact in the corresponding systems.

- Configuring replication between producing and consuming domains. This command will require orchestration of multiple domain agents from producing and consuming domains (1) granting access to the streaming data product to the consuming domain, (2) checking the capacity of both streaming platforms in each domain, and (3) provisioning the replication in the consuming domain from the producing domain.

- Publishing streaming data products involves (1) building the AsyncAPI YAML document, (2) registering its schema in the schema registry, (3) adding its deployment in the OpenLineage graph, and then (4) deploying the AsyncAPI in the streaming data catalog.

These workflows are themselves also not exhaustive. We will provide more detailed examples of these workflows and how to implement them later in this chapter.

In Figure 7-13 we illustrate the location of the domain agent as the agent/sidecar in each of the domains. The agent enables data movement to other domains in what is called the data plane in the streaming data mesh. The control plane controls the agents and orchestrates workflows on behalf of the management plane.

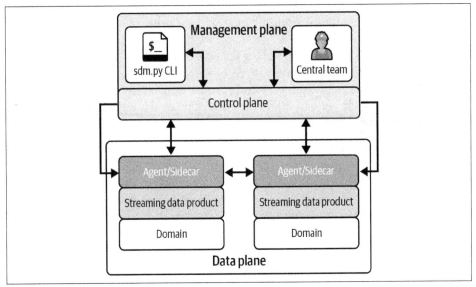

Figure 7-13. The planes in a streaming data mesh

We will refer to Figure 7-13 throughout this section and describe the data plane and control plane in detail.

Data Plane

In Figure 7-13, as stated previously, the data plane represents the domains replicating streaming data products between each other and supported by the domain agent. The domain agents take instructions from the control plane to configure the replication of data.

The agents configure the data replication mechanism. In this chapter, the mechanism we will use is cluster linking, which is a feature that enables Kafka brokers (by Confluent) to replicate between themselves. Configuration must include security as well as monitoring. The domains will not know the mechanism by which streaming data products are replicated to consuming domains or how the mechanism is secured.

Security logs (like audit logs) and usage metric logs from all the systems in the domain also are part of the data plane. Metric logs are sent to observability services like Datadog, AppDynamics, or Prometheus and Grafana. Security logs are sent to security information and event management (SIEM) services like Splunk, Sumo Logic, or SolarWinds. Many of these log services can be used for both metric logs and security logs. The domain agents configure these log systems automatically and are mostly hidden from the domains.

Control Plane

The *control plane* communicates with the domain agent to do many domain-related tasks. These tasks are initiated from the management plane by either the CLI or the central team. For more than half of this book, we have been referring to this part of the streaming data mesh as "the streaming data mesh" or even "the central domain." It holds the central team, the implementations of the self-services, and the systems that support the domains like OpenLineage and Schema Registry. As stated earlier, for the remainder of this book, we will call it the control plane. In Figure 7-14 the control plane holds three subplanes:

Metadata and registry plane
> Holds many of the open source tools that the control needs to use. They include OpenLineage, Apicurio, Schema Registry, and JFrog (an artifact repository). These tools hold much of the metadata consumers need in order to trust the streaming data products published in the streaming data mesh.

Management plane
> Provides access for users to monitor the streaming data mesh as well as to initiate commands.

Self-service plane

The self-service plane has the domain-facing services.

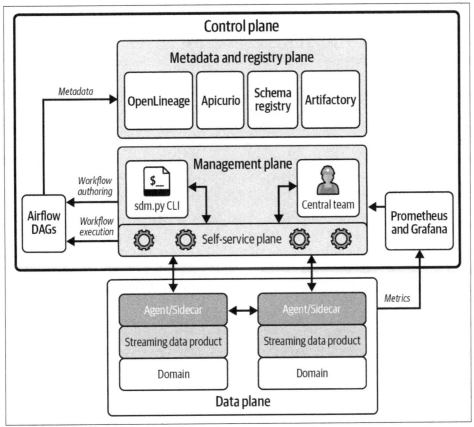

Figure 7-14. The control plane including its subplanes: metadata and registry plane, management plane, and self-service plane

What we have been calling "the central team" or "centralized systems" will now be called the streaming data mesh's control plane or just the control plane.

The management plane and metadata and registry plane

The management plane in Figure 7-14 provides the interfaces that are needed for domain personas to interact with their own domain through the control plane. The management plane also is used by the central team to manage the control plane as well as the domains. It contains visualizations that allow the team to monitor usage metrics and security logs. They are able to receive alerts from the logs and metrics to help diagnose issues. The central team is able to disable systems, sever connections, quarantine domains, and apply rate-limiting rules like throttling data throughput and storage.

The metadata and registry plane, which could actually be part of the management plane, allows users to manage schemas, monitor data product deployments, visualize lineage graphs, and update connectors/UDFs in JFrog Artifactory. We separate these planes in the illustration to again help organize the systems. A single visualization would help provide a "single pane of glass" to aggregate all the metadata and user interfaces needed to assist with managing the streaming data mesh in its entirety. You should be able to swap out different products for any of the systems in the management and metadata/registry plane and still get the same perspective of the streaming data mesh.

Self-service plane

The self-service plane does not have a visualization. It is the microsevices that implement the self-services that face the domains. It is also the microservices that control the streaming data mesh by the central team. These services directly communicate with the domain agents as well as invoke workflows. Basically, the self-service plane is made up of code developed by the central team to integrate all the domains and systems in the streaming data mesh.

Workflow orchestration.   Much of the code written in the self-service plane is implemented as workflow orchestration DAGs. These DAGs provide visualizations of the workflow that can be provided to regulation auditors and administrators of the central team. The visualizations are proof that data governance and regulations are being followed. For example, when building replication processes between producing and consuming domains, logic should be included to show that GDPR isn't being violated. It could be a machine learning algorithm that samples the data for sensitive information and denies replication. Or it can be a manual task enabling a security team member to do the same. Either way, seeing that a task is part of the workflow will help reassure everyone taking part in the streaming data mesh.

In Figure 7-14 the implementation of the workflow orchestration is Apache Airflow. Other workflow orchestrators in the market like Dagster and Luigi can do the same. In this example we will be using Airflow.

Implementing a DAG for linking.   Figure 7-15 is a DAG that shows the workflow for linking a producing domain with a consuming domain to replicate a streaming data product. In this example, a node in the DAG checks for GDPR violations. Figure 7-15 shows that GDPR regulation checks resulted in no violations, but for some there was a failure to grant access to the topic.

Figure 7-15. A DAG workflow that fails to grant access to a topic

We could add more logic to the DAG to check for more information that might affect creating a cluster link between domains. In Figure 7-16 we add two more nodes before actually granting access to a topic. First, we add a check to see if the destination Kafka cluster has the capacity to hold the streaming data product. Second, we check the capacity of the source Kafka cluster to see if it has the resources to add another consumer to its streaming data product.

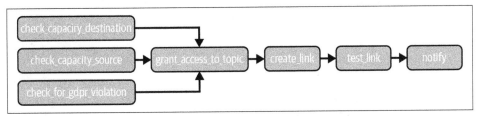

Figure 7-16. Adding more granularity to the workflow in the DAG

Being more precise in the representation of the workflow will help auditors know that we are taking the steps to protect against violations. Precision also provides easier debugging when commands are not working. Central teams can go directly to the specific task behind a workflow to investigate and resolve issues.

In Airflow, DAGs are written in Python. Example 7-2 is a snippet of Python code that shows how to assemble the DAG but lacks the implementation with the tasks. Each method is a task and provides input to the next task. This provides information for Airflow to introspect the code to generate a graphical view to users.

Example 7-2. Logging in to the streaming data mesh

```
1 @dag(
2       tags=['link'],
3       description='link data product to consuming domain'
4 )
5 def link():
6
7       @task
8       def grant_access_to_topic(data_product, source, destination):
9               return {}
10
11      @task
12      def check_capacity_source(destination):
13              return {}
14
```

```
15      @task
16      def check_capacity_destination(destination):
17              return {}
18
19      @task
20      def check_for_gdpr_violation(dataproduct):
21              return { "ok": True }
22
23      @task
24      def create_link(data_product, destination):
25              return {}
26
27      @task
28      def test_link(context):
29              return {}
30
31      @task
32      def notify(results):
33              return {}
34
35      data_product = "foo"
36      destination_domain = "bar"
37
38      result = check_for_gdpr_violation(data_product)
39      link = create_link(
40              grant_access_to_topic(
41                      result,
42                      check_capacity_source(destination_domain),
43                      check_capacity_destination(destination_domain)
44              ),
45              destination_domain
46      )
47      notify(test_link(link))
48
49
50 link = link()
```

This DAG should be customized to the business's data governance needs. The business may need additional tasks in the workflow, like capturing metric logs to be sent to Prometheus or adding more capacity in cases where that can be automatic. More importantly, it's necessary to make an OpenLineage call to append the consuming domain to the end of the lineage graph.

In Airflow, DAGs can also be triggered to start from an event (called Sensors) or invoked from a microservice, passing it all the parameters needed for the DAG to work. Although a streaming data mesh focuses on real-time use cases, the DAGs themselves don't need to be real-time and can run with batch semantics, especially if a workflow requires human intervention, like notifications and approvals. These human interventions will most likely occur the next day.

Implementing a DAG for publishing data products. Another DAG that would be important to visualize is for publishing a streaming data product. This example again helps visualize the steps you need to take to do this properly. In Figure 7-17 some of this workflow logic can become more complicated. Consider breaking it into multiple DAGs to simplify the visualization.

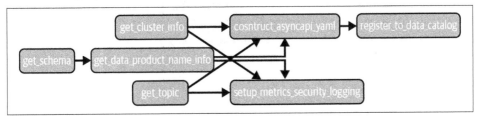

Figure 7-17. Publishing a streaming data product using a DAG

In this DAG, the important tasks are setting up logging and constructing the AsyncAPI YAML document. It's granular enough to help easily find issues with any of the tasks.

Infrastructure as code (IaC). Alternatively, you can incorporate within our DAGs code that calls tools like Terraform or Ansible that can build infrastructure. These tools are used to ease the work for provisioning and elastic scaling (scaling up or down). Likewise, frameworks like Kubernetes will help simplify some of these tasks related to the control plane.

Some examples of this would be deploying the streaming platform, the stream processing platform, and Kafka Connect. They can add additional brokers to increase the capacity of the streaming platform or add more Connect workers to the Kafka Connect cluster to handle larger loads. Building a hybrid of all these tools may help with provisioning infrastructure.

Summary

This chapter focused on how to build the data plane, the control plane (which includes additional subplanes), the self-service plane, and the management plane. We also provided some applications and tools to use to make this easy. We are not married to any of the products in our solutions. They are just a way to identify the parts that will help build a good control plane. The tools you eventually use hopefully will satisfy the functions that you're replacing.

This chapter relies heavily on the ability to replicate data between Kafka clusters (or the streaming platform of your choice). The diagrams in this chapter imply the use of cluster linking provided by Confluent to replicate/mirror Kafka topics between clusters. You could also do this with MirrorMaker 2 (MM2), which is an open source data replication tool between Kafka clusters. Other streaming platforms may have their own solutions to replicating streaming data, which could include separating storage layers or using tiered storage. These details are beyond the scope of this book.

The central team does require deeper skills in coding and infrastructure. The data engineers that previously were working in the monolithic data lake or warehouse are perfect for transitioning to the central team. Some skills they should have are Python, Java/Scala, Kubernetes, Terraform, and building microservices. In Chapter 8, we will provide guidance for building a data team that will help you create a good streaming data mesh.

Building a Decentralized Data Team

Companies require a sound strategy in order to shift from an on-premises to a cloud-based architecture. Most companies have seen roles mature and become more specialized, particularly as they relate to data science, data engineering, and machine learning engineering. All of these specialties play a key role in working with data within the cloud ecosystem.

Additionally, the demand for data professionals has risen dramatically over the past few years. This, paired with a steady rate decline of new professionals who are educated in data infrastructure, creates a talent gap where there are not enough professionals to fill the demand for these roles. This gap has created an ongoing demand for software within the data infrastructure space (covered in Chapter 7) that can help with automating key tasks to ease the burden of filling the talent shortage.

Technology is capable of handling some of the existing gaps, but not all. As a result, businesses need to find alternatives to boosting productivity with existing skill sets. As these skill sets are in high demand, additional hiring and staff augmentation are often not an option. Building a decentralized data team helps fill this gap by moving resources within the organization to supply the skill sets necessary to support a streaming data mesh approach.

In this chapter we will review the traditional approach to data, some of its pitfalls, and contrast this with a new approach to aligning resources to data. This new approach combines business and technical expertise into a structure that supports developing high-quality data products that align with business objectives.

The Traditional Data Warehouse Structure

Data engineering roles were traditionally performed by someone who knew SQL on the database side, MapReduce on the big data ecosystem, and generally understood how to move data in batches from the operational plane to the data warehouse. As machine learning and data science have become more prevalent in recent years, the data engineer's role has become more burdensome. And these roles have become more monolithic, and more focused on areas such as DevOps, MLOps, data science, and ML engineering. Thus, the standard term "data engineer" has now become very overloaded, and new roles need to be created. As we look at building a decentralized team, we will introduce these new roles and discuss their overall impact on the team.

Figure 8-1 depicts a typical organization structure in a data warehousing environment. Two teams roll up under the C-suite:

- The operational team that supports day-to-day operations
- The team that manages a data warehouse in the data plane

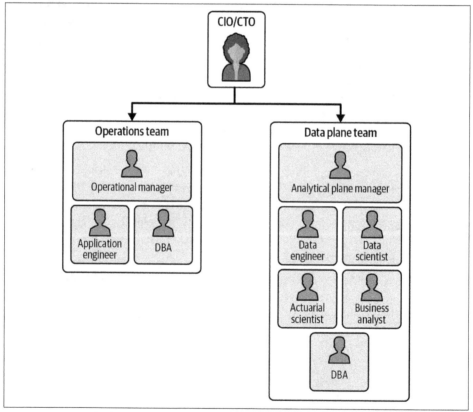

Figure 8-1. Sample data warehouse organizational structure

In a typical data warehouse project, the goal is to bring the data from its operational source to the data plane, and then restructure this data into another form. The Behavioral Insights, Data Science, and Analytics teams, not depicted here, build content from this centralized data warehouse.

This approach is all too common and has a number of pitfalls. A recent study shows that some 80% of these data warehouses fail to fulfill the objectives that they set out to achieve. Some of the reasons cited deal with aspects of the data (dirty data, data silos, data access, regulatory restrictions, etc.), yet one of the main contributors to the problem is found in the organizational structure itself. In its simplest form, the data warehouse organization, data engineers, and ETL developers are brought in to take data from the operational stores and load it into a new table structure using a new technology. These people often find themselves working with data that is unknown to them, and they initially lack the business context to understand the data's usage, as well as the knowledge of how the originating transactional system works.

This leads to many meetings between the business and operations teams to determine requirements for bringing this data into the data warehouse. The data engineering team, typically a subset of the data plane team, then takes on the burden of creating a data structure that will satisfy all users, often making key design decisions in silos where cardinality and distribution are changed or the original meaning of a data set changes from what it originally represented. These data structures may become overgeneralized and do not fit the exact needs of business users.

As the data warehouse project progresses, business must continue as usual. This means that operational reports are still generated from the transactional operational database, with the intent to move these activities to the data warehouse upon its completion. Data scientists typically have their own processes (and often their own data engineers) in place to get data that meets their requirements. Once the data warehouse project is completed, users often find that cardinality and distribution have changed, and data is not shaped in a familiar pattern. Also, permissions come into play: teams that once had access to data needed for their daily tasks are prohibited from querying the data warehouse (or the tables in the data warehouse) for "security reasons."

These issues, and others, cause teams to find workarounds and alternative feeds in order to circumvent the data repository. The goal of an organization to create one managed, single-source version of the truth in data often becomes obscured and fragmented. In reality, an organization begins to create many sources of truth, each with its own "independent" ETL and data engineering steps. In more severe instances, teams have also been known to set up their own infrastructure to create and maintain shadow copies of transactional data, leading to even more concerns around security and data quality.

Introducing the Decentralized Team Structure

In Figure 8-2 we introduce the concept of the decentralized team. This structure has many of the same resources as in the data warehouse organization but reorganizes these roles to more closely relate to three areas: (1) data expertise, (2) business expertise, and (3) infrastructure expertise and data transformation as it relates to the control plane.

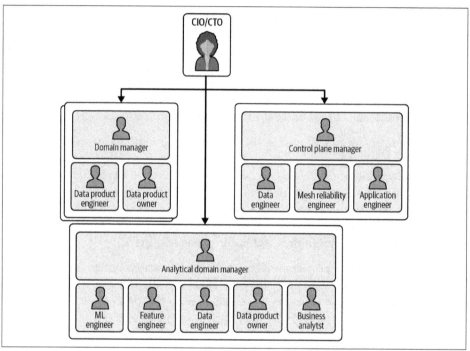

Figure 8-2. Sample decentralized data team structure

In this new mesh structure, the entire organization is moved closer to the data itself, making resources within a domain align directly with the data that is provided to business users. In streaming data mesh, the domain team is responsible for all aspects of data within a domain, including creation, ingestion, preparation, and making the data available. Federating ownership by domain allows the business to maintain each domain's original context since teams know their data very well. The responsibility of the domain team shifts away from the central infrastructure team and is laser focused on providing valuable data products to the organization.

A critical feature of a decentralized data team is the need to shift from a traditional centralized approach to an end-to-end process, to one where data products become the focal point among multiple organizational skill sets that deliver valued outcomes. Decentralized organizations will identify well-defined competency homes for their team members who have served traditional technology roles: architects, analysts, and data engineers. Team performance is more appropriately measured and rewarded according to their work as part of a dedicated domain team. Teams become multidisciplined as data product development teams are formed to address key organizational needs (and their ability to add value as they move from one team to another). These decentralized domain teams, while dedicated to the content within their domain, allow the business to think from the lens of the consumer, ensuring that quality is put first and that data products address customer requirements (in this case, data consumers in other domains).

The principle of domain ownership further bolsters the second principle of data mesh: "data as a product." Because each domain owns its own data and is responsible for producing and developing data for its consumers, it is expected to be high quality, near-real-time, and trustworthy. Most importantly, data products and their domains must be reliable and trustworthy enough to be the source for domain interoperability for the creation of new data domains and products. The organizational mindset requires a dynamic shift from one that creates a centralized team to service all data requests, to one where data generated by one domain can be used by another. Let's take a look at four major areas of benefit to a decentralized data team: empowering people, working processes, fostering collaboration, and data-driven automation.

Empowering People

Developing a decentralized data team has a significant impact on almost every aspect of the organization, including structures, roles, responsibilities, business vocabulary, processes, collaboration models, and technology. Product owners ensure that domain consumers are at the center of product development. They need to be given authority to make key decisions and engage directly with customers to avoid unnecessary roadblocks. Direct customer interaction ensures clear communication of requirements and priorities into the domain development process, which in turn drives agility, increased productivity, and consumer satisfaction.

Leaders will need to adapt, as some roles go from front-line leadership of projects to managing capabilities that add value as part of domain developments led by product owners. Team members will need to understand their specific roles and adapt to working more flexibly across a range of projects and leveraging their core skills to deliver value within their assigned domains.

As a decentralized team approach is adopted, senior leadership needs to actively and visibly lead the change in culture. A sound leader must identify, agree on, and adopt the values and behaviors required for this data-focused culture. Leaders need to challenge and confront behaviors that interfere with collaboration among traditionally centralized teams to ensure they work within domains to deliver the greatest value for the organization by serving consumers as its customer base.

Working Processes

In decentralized teams, new products and services are developed in close interaction with end consumers—the customer—and ideas and prototypes are field tested early in the development process so teams can quickly gather feedback on improvements. Doing this takes engagement and relationship skills. Standardized processes deployed within functions, across multiple regions and with a common ubiquitous language, enable teams to communicate clearly with one another, increasing both mobility and scaling. Virtually moving people between geographies to add value where it is most needed can produce a global impact when changing demands require rapid action and solutions. Teams need measurable performance goals for processes to help track customer satisfaction and to determine how processes can be improved. Team members should be encouraged to experiment and iterate to seek ways of improving process and customer outcomes. "Fail fast" is encouraged, while an entrepreneurial spirit is supported (and rewarded) throughout the organization.

Fostering Collaboration

When you create a decentralized team, fostering strong collaboration among teams needs to be addressed from the outset. Strong product owners who can mobilize multiskilled teams around cross-cutting value propositions are critical to this process. Product owners need to have sufficient knowledge to work with and understand issues raised by team members from diverse groups such as IT, Sales, Marketing, and Data Delivery. Transparency of information and data becomes even more critical if self-managed teams are to identify ongoing improvements and share knowledge across teams.

Data-Driven Automation

Advanced analytics enables data-driven automation. Through sophisticated technology, an organization can automatically discern insights and make recommendations. This technology provides intelligence to improve decision making and can be applied to many aspects of a business. Digital tools can transform the journey from operational data to data product by reconstructing the process of turning data discovery into a data product. *Robotic process automation* (RPA) is an emerging technology that can replace human effort in processes that involve aggregating data from multiple systems. In addition, models built by data scientists and machine learning experts can now be developed, deployed, and maintained in real time. While these tools can be used in a traditional data architecture, the decentralized team approach allows the domain team to deploy these tools to improve product delivery within these subject areas. Since the decentralized team is responsible for the scope of the domain it services, automated tools can be used to address specific problems rather than applying them to the broader scope of the entire data set.

Several aspects of data as a product need to be understood before we explain the new roles. Here is a brief overview of these principles. As we introduce new roles, we will illustrate these data-as-product aspects:

- A domain can have one or more data products.
- Data products need to be interoperable. They can consume outputs from other data products and produce their own output. Multiple data products that use one another will form a data mesh of products.
- The technical implementation, such as sourcing data, data modeling, and ETL, will be abstracted under the data product. The data product team itself will be empowered to design and implement the technical solution at the domain level.
- Some data products will be aligned with operational source systems. Some data products will consume output from source-aligned data products as well as other data products to generate value-added output.
- Some data products will be aligned with specific business needs, such as behavioral insight reporting or data science.

New Roles in Data Domains

The major shift in the way an organization thinks about its data requires certain new roles to be created within the domain. The most important of these is the *domain product owner*. This role is responsible for (1) creating the vision and road map of data products, (2) ensuring consumer satisfaction and the data products' utility within the organization, and (3) ensuring availability, quality, and traceability, and maintaining service levels.

Data engineering roles are a necessity in data mesh, but not in the traditional sense. For streaming use cases, standard SQL and ETL are replaced with transformations using the KStream API with Kotlin as the workhorse, or with tools like ksqlDB. The data engineer now has to understand how to properly work within this paradigm to apply data transformation to streaming sets rather than relational tables. As we move through this section, it is implied that the data engineer is understood to be a *domain data engineer*. While the source and targets that a data engineer services are different, the role is very much the same: an operational source of data is available for consumption from a streaming data source, and transformed data is published into a data product that serves the consumer. This requires skills in data transformation, as well as a solid background in designing and creating standardized, versioned APIs that can be published to a central repository as data products.

New Roles in the Data Plane

One of the advantages of data mesh and streaming data mesh is that these shift the responsibility to make data available away from the central infrastructure team. This allows the infrastructure team to focus on creating reliable, usable, and tangible self-service assets to empower domain teams. While the domain team focuses on accessing data and its transformations, infrastructure and self-service tools are managed by the *data plane team*.

The data plane team is composed of data experts and *data plane data engineers*, who are familiar with source systems and are capable of managing the infrastructure around publishing these via connectors to the streaming data mesh. This role is responsible for reliable, performant, and scalable connectivity from transactional sources, and publishing this to domains. This role creates standard input and output interfaces from source systems, and these can be in the form of streams or APIs.

The *mesh reliability engineer* role is concentrated on just that—the overall performance and reliability of the mesh. This is done by monitoring, maintaining, and reacting to performance and utilization metrics of the mesh deployment. The person in this role may be responsible for expanding or managing tiered storage, scaling data products horizontally, and reporting usage metrics back to domain managers and product owners. Additionally, this role is responsible for the overall deployment stability. For instance, if data products are deployed on Kubernetes, streams can also be deployed on Kubernetes. The mesh reliability engineer ensures that processing is reliable and can happen on a Kubernetes-based cluster.

Streaming data mesh is a self-service platform, majorly focused around people and tools. This introduces the role of the *application engineer*. New tools are required that provide a simple user interface to define and register events and event schemas, provision a streaming platform, provide CLI interfaces to provision data streaming pipelines, and test transformation scripts. A person in this role serves on a highly skilled team that builds and maintains the toolset used by the domain team, as well as tools that serve the team supporting the control plane. Creating these tools will decrease the need for maintaining a highly skilled control team over time. This being said, eventually this team could be composed largely of generalists with a small set of specialists.

Also, the application engineer role is responsible for maintaining and deploying the technology underneath operational and analytical applications. This includes popular tools such as Jupyter notebooks, and libraries such as TensorFlow, XGBoost, Keras, and PyTorch that facilitate model training.

New Roles in Data Science and Business Intelligence

Streaming data mesh is intended to serve as the intermediary layer between streaming technology and data science. As a result, many roles emerge as a necessity to feed analytical models and feature stores. With all the roles being defined, the data science team will play a large role because of its exposure to statistics and its proper application. Josh Wills, a data science and software engineering expert, defined a scientist as a "person who is better at statistics than any software engineer, and better at software engineering than any statistician." This definition really captures the true nature of what the modern-day data scientist does on a daily basis. A data scientist is typically not an optimal software engineer, nor is this person a 100% statistician. Yet the data scientist needs to know enough about all aspects of the process to do the following:

- *Consolidate* the proper data for a model
- *Transform* this data into a useful format for building models
- *Apply* appropriate statistical preprocessing steps to data
- *Select* an appropriate algorithm to use for predicting outcomes
- *Understand* the target deployment platform

This is a tall order. A true data scientist has to be able to effectively (not optimally) apply knowledge in these areas in order to present results to the business for evaluation, while understanding all the operational components that fit underneath this umbrella concept of data science. This data scientist needs to understand how to effectively apply ETL techniques to consolidate data and transform this data into a useful format for the model.

Many of the tasks performed by the data scientist are better suited for a data engineer. However, a generalist data engineer may not be well versed in how a data scientist wants this data to be organized. This creates a new a new role, the *data science engineer*, or *machine learning engineer*.

The data scientist needs to apply appropriate statistical preprocessing steps to data generated when the data is first consolidated and transformed. This requires an additional role that is much more specialized than a data engineer but not quite to the level of the data scientist. This role, which can be served by the *data science engineer*, can also be split out into the new role, the *feature process engineer*. Under the guidance of a data scientist, these feature process engineers understand the required data transformations and are technically adept at implementing them within the data mesh.

Data setup for a model is often an overlooked aspect of the entire process and is often considered a magical black box that requires little attention. In the mind of most business people, data goes into the model, and results emerge. In reality, this is a complex process that requires much thought and attention.

Categorical variables, which are often blindly fed into a one-hot encoding transformation (the process of converting categorical variables into a vector of zeros and ones for each combination that occurs), is often overused and can be both ineffective in predicting outcomes as well as inefficient (and quite often computationally impossible) in model training and model inference. Categorical variables often require the proper application of dimensionality reduction, and many techniques exist that can be applied to categorical variables, such as these:

- Target encoding
- Trained embeddings using a deep learning framework
- Principal component analysis (PCA)

Furthermore, any type of dimensionality reduction needs to be explainable in human terms for business analysts and end consumers.

PCA, for instance, is extremely difficult to explain past the first two principal components. Trained embeddings are also difficult (albeit easier) to explain. Target encoding, in its simplest form, is the probability relationship between a categorical value and its known outcomes. While being able to explain these transformations is important, it is also important to pick the proper approach for the model being built. As a data scientist defines what type(s) of variable encoding a model requires, the feature process engineer must understand how to implement this solution.

Just as categorical variables need proper treatment, so does numerical input. Data in a continuous variable often needs to be standardized or normalized (both are entirely different concepts) to properly train models. Some model frameworks handle this automatically (such as XGBoost), while others do not. Also, geographic coordinates, while numeric, often require special handling since there is a known distance relationship between these data points. With data science (and often statistical) guidance, proper transformations can be applied to data to best fit the model.

And finally, output variables need to be considered in transformation, depending on the desired outcome of the model. For instance, if a model is being trained to find anomalous insurance claims, the dependent (or outcome variable) may need to be expressed in standardized terms so that the distance between actual and predicted can be measured in units of standard deviation. Also, the dependent variable in any model typically needs to be representative of a Gaussian distribution, so that the model does not have to computationally struggle to find relationships. With the direction of the data scientist, the feature process engineer can optimally orchestrate and apply proper engineering techniques to produce the required model inputs.

While the data scientist or machine learning practitioner needs to be able to apply the proper model, another important facet extends the concept of DevOps, creating the *MLOps* role. This role takes the model, with all the artifacts produced in the model building phase, and creates a pipeline that properly applies all required transformations for proper real-time and batch inference. While the model training process developed by the data scientist and feature process engineer has an obligation to bundle up its transformations with the model itself (along with fit statistics and potentially other relevant values), *MLOps* must apply these transformations in an equivalent fashion to model training. Cases of never-before-seen values, too, need to be handled appropriately under the guidance of the data scientist.

The term *pipeline* has recently become very overloaded in both MLOps and data science. In the case of model building and inference, there is the data transformation pipeline, as well as the model deployment pipeline. The deployment pipeline itself can typically be built using standard Agile processes and deployed with common-place tools such as Jenkins or Azure DevOps.

When deploying a model, its associated transformations must be published to the data lineage repository and documented as known transformations. This takes the guesswork out of what transformations have been applied and their potential impact on results. In any case, understanding the steps that a model takes must be transparent and viewable to any and all users that consume the model.

The *business intelligence engineer* is another role, one that requires a mixture of data source knowledge from the operational plane with analytic data product exposure as produced by the data science team. In this role, a mixture of data science and generalized streaming data engineer skills are required. Over time, the control plane team may create tools that automate some of this integration, alleviating the need for a specialist role.

Table 8-1 provides a summary of these roles. The alignment of roles is a suggestion only. This is customizable for individual business requirements.

Table 8-1. Decentralized data team roles

Role-defined area	Role
Domain	Domain manager
Domain	Data product owner
Domain	Streaming data engineer
Control plane	Control plane manager
Control plane	Data engineer
Control plane	Mesh reliability engineer

Role-defined area	Role
Control plane	Application engineer
Analytics	Analytical domain manager
Analytics	Analytical product owner
Analytics	Business analyst
Analytics	ML engineer
Feature engineer	Streaming data engineer

In conclusion, by embedding these roles within domain teams, a domain team becomes self-sufficient to develop, deploy, and maintain its data products. Engineers, analysts, SMEs, and technology experts are able to collaborate in creating world-class data products and solutions. While one is an expert on technology, another is an expert on business context. An empowered data product culture pushes responsibility to the empowered, autonomous teams that have objectives to be met. Business objectives are still set from the C-suite, but the decision-making and solutioning process becomes local to the autonomous team.

CHAPTER 9

Feature Stores

As we previously mentioned, the ETL process pulls data from operational data stores (which power the applications that serve the business), and feeds that data into the analytical data plane. The analytical plane is used to build statistical models that drive insights, which the business then uses to make critical decisions. These decisions are fed back to the operational plane to improve and optimize performance and ultimately increase revenue. One of the principles of a data product in a data mesh is to provide high-quality and trustable data to analytical teams. Quality and trustability help build confidence in analytical outcomes.

Features, or *columns*, are measurable pieces of data like height, width, age, weight, amount, and price that can be used for analysis. *Feature engineering* is the process of extracting and preparing data for analytical processing and storing it into a feature store. The *feature store* serves prepared analytical data to data scientists. Before the advent of feature stores, data scientists and engineers worked together in a very disoriented and disorganized approach when building insights. Often, data was hard to locate and unclean. Its freshness was unknown, its source was often questionable, and its compliance with data governance was unclear. This made insights derived from this data less trustworthy, less certain, and hard to repeat. These are just a few of the issues that manifest when working within a monolithic data lake or warehouse.

Data scientists needed a better way to access prepared analytical data, and data engineers needed a repeatable way of preparing data for data scientists. The feature store and feature engineering brought an organized approach to the process of sourcing analytical data. The responsibility to create data sets to repeat model runs and experiments was also placed on data engineers, which required a framework to capture and store historical analytical data.

The feature store registers its data in a feature catalog similar to a data catalog. The feature store provides the metadata needed to bring confidence and trustability to the analytical data used for inference. This is where a data mesh naturally fits with feature engineering, by allowing feature stores to acquire the metadata that comes with published data products. Features also automatically inherit the full data lineage and documentation that come with the data product. The feature store separates the data engineer from the data scientist and creates a better framework and API for each to work in.

In this chapter we will talk about online and offline data stores, Apache Feast (and how to extend this framework to support streaming data mesh), and the roles required for supporting the data science organization.

Separating Data Engineering from Data Science

Data preparation accounts for about 80% of the work of data scientists.
    —Gil Press, "Cleaning Big Data: Most Time-Consuming, Least Enjoyable Data Science Task, Survey Says," *Forbes*, March 2016

Figure 9-1 shows that the amount of time spent on preparing data for analytics is significant enough that data engineers should be dedicated to this task. Data preparation is a task more aligned with data engineering, and the burden of preparing data for analytics should not be placed on the data science team.

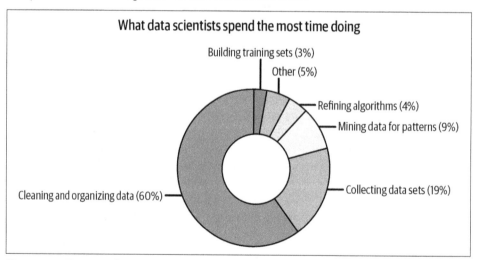

Figure 9-1. Estimated time spent on data preparation (from Forbes)

Data scientists should spend their time on experimenting and implementing models, tuning hyperparameters, and selecting features rather than preparing data. We recommend that data cleansing and organization be delegated to data engineers, allowing data scientists to focus on activities that align with their specialty. The feature store allows this separation of tasks.

The feature store organizes the way data scientists and data engineers work together by creating a framework that separates them (ironically). Data scientists can load features from a feature store without ever having to contact the data engineer. This provides the data scientists the time and capability to iterate through their analytics faster, delivering insights faster to the business. Also, since the feature store has each feature's metadata, the insights become more trustworthy, creating more confidence in business decisions.

For the data engineer, a new responsibility now evolves that requires them to source data and prepare it to be easily accessible to the data science team. As we noted previously, this is called feature engineering. Feature engineering, using a feature store, provides a "write once" approach when preparing features since it negates the need to re-create the same pipeline for different time windows.

Example 9-1 shows one way a data scientist interfaces with the feature store. Data scientists are now able to load prepared features without the need to reach out to the data engineer. Once the data engineer understands the requirements of a feature, the data engineer owns the responsibility of preparing features.

Example 9-1. Data scientist fetching feature vectors for inference from a feature store; perspective is from a notebook

```
store = FeatureStore(repo_path=".")

feature_vector = store.get_online_features(
    features=[
        "click_users:views",
        "click_users:url",
        "click_users:duration",
    ],
    entity_rows=[
        # {join_key: entity_value}
        {"userid": 1004},
        {"userid": 1005},
    ],
).to_dict()
```

On the data engineering side, data engineers can source their data from real-time streaming platforms, prepare the features, and then load them into online and offline data stores that are part of the feature store.

Online and Offline Data Stores

In a feature store, there are online and offline stores. *Offline stores* contain data sets that live in a database, data warehouse, or data lake. *Online data stores* contain data stored in an in-memory database like Redis, MongoDB, or Cassandra. The online store is used for low-latency scoring use cases, and the offline store is used for training and batch scoring. An example of an offline store is any data lake with Apache Hive or Spark as the query engine.

The offline and online stores are merged in a Lambda architecture so that the feature store can serve the most recent features (calculated from the most recent data), as well as their historical values to allow data scientists to repeat experiments and model runs.

The best way to understand how a streaming data mesh can help improve the analytical plane when serving features is to look at an existing open source feature store. Let's look at Apache Feast to illustrate the benefits of a feature store.

Apache Feast Introduction

Apache Feast is an open source feature store originally built by Uber as part of the Michelangelo project and contributed to the Apache Software Foundation.

The architectural diagram of the Apache Feast feature store (*https://feast.dev*) is shown in Figure 9-2. On the left of the diagram, data is sourced from streams and data stores. The data is merged to build a real-time and historical view of the data. The architecture is inspired by the Lambda architecture we described in Chapter 2. The merged data is transformed into features and saved into the feature store. The feature store then serves the features for model training and real-time inference (scoring).

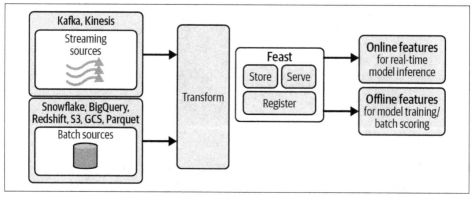

Figure 9-2. Apache Feast architecture diagram (from feast.dev)

In Chapter 2 we also talked about the differences between Lambda and Kappa architectures. Whereas Lambda merges streaming and batch sources, Kappa is a simplified architecture that requires only streaming. Figure 9-3 is an example of a Feast architecture in which the data is sourced solely from the stream but populates both online and offline stores. This architecture still needs to merge the offline store with the online store to create the real-time and historical data in the feature store.

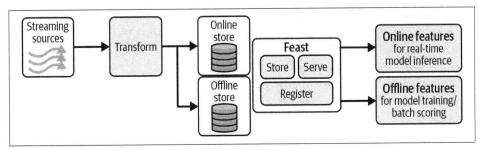

Figure 9-3. Preprocessing for Lambda architecture

An alternative architecture using Apache Feast is illustrated in Figure 9-4. This diagram shows only an online store from which both real-time and historical data is served from the feature store. The online store needs to be able to hold historical and real-time data as well as serve it with low latency. The advantage is that merging between online and offline stores is no longer necessary, and the feature store is easier to implement since it eliminates the need for an offline store. The disadvantage is it places significant responsibility on the online store, which makes this solution less optimal for large amounts of historical data. If a use case requires only three months of data for training, for example, then the type of architecture shown in Figure 9-4 may be better suited since long-living historical features are not required.

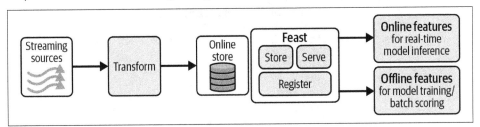

Figure 9-4. Kappa feature store implementation

Enabling a Kappa architecture requires extending Apache Feast so that the transformation logic and storage database can be swapped out with inline stream transformation and storage of offline features.

Apache Feast allows the ability to swap out its default implementation through a *provider*. Providers allow feature engineers to change how data is materialized, swap out the storage database, change how data transformed, and change how data is optimized for reading.

A provider is a Python application that changes the default streaming and batch implementation. Data then gets loaded into Apache Feast, and the pipeline is executed using overriding operations. Example 9-2 shows a template of a provider.

To implement a Kappa architecture with Apache Feast, a provider needs to be created that implements the streaming and batching work in the stream processing framework of your choice. In the `materialize_single_feature_view` function, instead of reading from an offline store and executing a batch job, data needs to be read from an online store. Example 9-2 shows a diagram of Kappa architecture as depicted in Figure 9-4.

Example 9-2. Apache Feast provider example

```python
from datetime import datetime
from typing import Any, Callable, Dict, List, Optional, Sequence, Tuple, Union
from feast.entity import Entity
from feast.feature_table import FeatureTable
from feast.feature_view import FeatureView
from feast.infra.local import LocalProvider
from feast.infra.offline_stores.offline_store import RetrievalJob
from feast.protos.feast.types.EntityKey_pb2 import EntityKey as EntityKeyProto
from feast.protos.feast.types.Value_pb2 import Value as ValueProto
from feast.infra.registry.registry import Registry
from feast.repo_config import RepoConfig

class SDMCustomProvider(LocalProvider):
    def __init__(self, config: RepoConfig, repo_path):
        super().__init__(config)
        # Add your custom init code here. This code runs on every Feast operation.

    def update_infra(
        self,
        project: str,
        tables_to_delete: Sequence[Union[FeatureTable, FeatureView]],
        tables_to_keep: Sequence[Union[FeatureTable, FeatureView]],
        entities_to_delete: Sequence[Entity],
        entities_to_keep: Sequence[Entity],
        partial: bool,
    ):
        super().update_infra(
            project,
            tables_to_delete,
            tables_to_keep,
            entities_to_delete,
            entities_to_keep,
            partial,
        )
```
❶

```
def materialize_single_feature_view(
    self,
    config: RepoConfig,
    feature_view: FeatureView,
    start_date: datetime,
    end_date: datetime,
    registry: Registry,
    project: str,
    tqdm_builder: Callable[[int], tqdm],
) -> None:
    super().materialize_single_feature_view(
        config, feature_view, start_date, end_date, registry, project,
        tqdm_builder
    )
    ❷
```

❶ Implement your streaming work here.

❷ Change your batching work to streaming work.

Example 9-2 also shows how Apache Feast can change the online and offline stores by using a Python technique similar to what we saw in this example. Making the offline store the same as the online store should negate the requirement for merging between data stores. This approach will allow you to change only the stores and not how the data is processed.

Optionally, RTOLAP databases like Apache Druid and Apache Pinot are good alternative data stores that can be used as feature stores. RTOLAP databases can serve data at very low latencies, and depending on the amount of historical data, they could be an optimal choice. In most use cases, historical data will be served from a data warehouse or data lake because of its size. Training or serving skew can be minimized by utilizing the same transformation definitions as defined in the RTOLAP implementation for the processing of historical data, then synced to a data lake or data warehouse such as Snowflake.

Feature stores that consume from a streaming data product integrate seamlessly into a feature store, including Apache Feast. Metadata for the data products is inherited by the feature store. Data then ultimately becomes accessible to the data scientists who need the reliability, definition, and trustworthiness that the metadata brings to their analytics.

Real-time data and metadata that the streaming data mesh provides can offer significant benefits to feature stores and analytical use cases. These benefits include features that are calculated from data in real time and increased trustworthiness in data that is sourced. In Chapter 10 we will go over a simple example of a streaming data mesh.

Summary

ZD strictly ties the data mesh paradigm to analytical use cases. In this chapter, we showed how analytical tools like feature stores directly benefit from the data mesh. The data product metadata preserved by the data mesh provides a complete history of the data that eventually will get transformed into features served to the data scientists.

CHAPTER 10

Streaming Data Mesh in Practice

In this final chapter, we will walk through the ideas proposed in the previous chapters by looking at an example of a simple streaming data mesh. We will go through the experience of building streaming data products using data domains (a collection of values that are related to one subject area) as an example.

Figure 10-1 shows the streaming data mesh example that we will use in this chapter. The control plane in this example does not have all the components that appear in the latter part of Chapter 7. It includes only the necessary components to build, publish, and share streaming data products across domains:

- A schema registry
- Data lineage
- Airflow for ETL workflow execution
- A data management plane that includes a CLI for administration
- Components within the data domain that stream data into the management plane

In Figure 10-1, we have taken out the repository that holds libraries like Kafka connectors or UDFs since we will not be showing this use case. We've also removed the Confluent Schema Registry, replacing it with the schema registry that comes with Apicurio. The Confluent Schema Registry will come into play within the domains that we will cover in a later section. Lastly, we have omitted Prometheus and Grafana. This reduces the number of services and the resources needed to run them on the local computer.

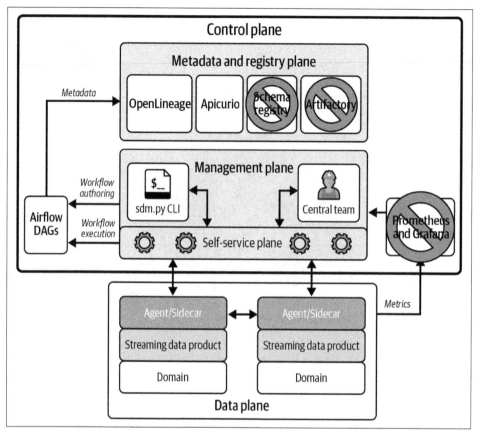

Figure 10-1. Simple streaming data mesh example without JFrog/Artifactory, Prometheus, and Grafana

Streaming Data Mesh Example

To summarize what you've learned in this book, a streaming data mesh is a data architecture that is:

- Built for generalist engineers in domains to build and publish data products
- Controlled by federated data governance
- Serviced by domain-facing self-services
- Implemented by hyper-skilled engineers

To get started, run the command in Example 10-1 to clone the example locally from GitHub.

Example 10-1. Simple streaming data mesh

```
git clone git@github.com:hdulay/streaming-data-mesh.git
```

In our example scenario, hyper-skilled engineers have designed and implemented a streaming data mesh. This includes the self-services, the domain agents, and Airflow workflows (DAGs). They completed a basic streaming data mesh—one that meets the minimum requirements of a streaming data mesh. In this scenario, the engineers have accomplished the following tasks.

In the producing domain:

1. Installed a connector that previously wasn't installed.

2. Deployed a connector to start producing two data sets for two topics in Kafka: clickstream data and user data. This data will be used to perform joins later.

3. Auto-created a table from the Kafka topics so that the domain engineer can start using the data within them in a SQL stream processing engine—either ksqlDB or a SaaS stream processor.

4. Deployed SQL that transforms and joins the two data sets.

5. Published the finished streaming data product for others to browse in Apicurio.

In the consuming domain:

1. Requested to consume a data product found in Apicurio.

2. Replicated the streaming data product to a Kafka cluster in the consuming domain.

In OpenLineage:

- Ensured that the lineage graph represents data capture from its source into the consuming domain and represents all steps in between, like SQL statements, connectors, topics, clusters, replication, etc.

In Apicurio:

- Enabled the capability to search for streaming data products and view their schemas.

This example will implement only the self-services that will accomplish the preceding use cases. Many more self-services are required to make this example a production-ready streaming data mesh, such as security, monitoring, and infrastructure provisioning that we've purposely omitted for simplicity.

We will perform each of these use cases against infrastructure running on premises that is self-managed and one that uses infrastructure that is fully managed in the cloud. We will start by deploying a simplistic on-premises streaming data mesh.

Deploying an On-Premises Streaming Data Mesh

As we did in previous chapters, we will use the CLI to perform all of our interactions in the streaming data mesh. After cloning the GitHub repository in Example 10-1, you will see a directory tree similar to the following:

```
streaming-data-mesh
|--airflow
|  |--dags
|--cli
|--confluent
|  |--docker-compose.yaml
|--connect
|  |--clickstream.json
|  |--user.json
|  |--debezium.postgres.json
|--control-plane
|--domain-agent
|--marquez
|--modules
|--sql
|  |--cleanse.sql
|  |--join.sql
|--Makefile
```

 This directory tree may change in the future as it evolves.

The CLI is located in the *cli* directory. It supports both the on-premises (self-managed) and cloud (fully managed) versions of our streaming data mesh example. A *Makefile* in the home directory helps with starting the services that are part of the control plane of the streaming data mesh, as well as the infrastructure within the domains.

The *confluent* directory holds a *docker-compose.yaml* file that starts up the components of Confluent Platform, which contains the following:

- Two single-node Kafka and ZooKeeper clusters, one for each domain
- Single-node Kafka Connect cluster
- Single-node ksqlDB cluster

- Single-node Confluent Schema Registry
- Single-node Confluent REST Proxy

All services are assumed to be running within the domain's on-premises infrastructure. In our example, the domain looks like Figure 10-2. In previous chapters, we did not talk about the existence of a *Schema Registry* or *REST Proxy* in a domain. The Schema Registry in the domain will be there to manage schemas that the domain doesn't want exposed outside. Instead, Apicurio in the control plane will be used to manage public schemas between domains.

The REST Proxy serves as a proxy to Kafka and is needed when we are assembling metadata required for our streaming data products and provisioning cluster links between domains.

The Confluent components, including the REST Proxy and Schema Registry, are not exposed outside the domain, including the Connect cluster, Kafka, and ksqlDB. Any access to any services within the domain can be accomplished only through the domain agent. However, anything within the domain can reach out to any services it needs, including the control plane.

> An alternative to the Confluent Schema Registry is Karapace, an open source alternative Schema Registry and REST Proxy.

The *domain-agent* directory contains an application that serves as the sidecar to the domain. Its responsibility is to control the replication of streaming data products between domains. In this case, we are using Confluent's cluster linking. Figure 10-2 illustrates the streaming services that the *domain agent* interacts with.

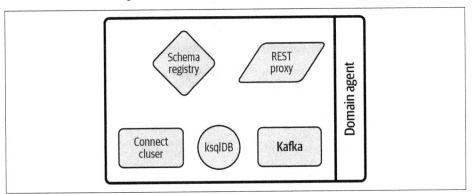

Figure 10-2. Simple streaming data mesh example domain diagram

Now that we have established the components within the data mesh, we need to establish a means to connect data lineage. We chose Marquez since it's an open source data lineage implementation. In the *marquez* directory is Marquez, which implements OpenLineage. The *modules* directory contains the shared common libraries used by the CLI, domain agent, and control plane. The *sql* directory contains the SQL statements we will use to transform the streaming data products. Lastly, the *Makefile* organizes all of the commands we will use in this chapter.

 If deploying in a cloud provider like AWS, you may consider a domain as being a virtual private cloud (VPC). Security groups can allow outbound connectivity from within the VPC, but expose the domain agent only for inbound requests from the control plane and cluster-linked domains.

To get started, you'll need to initialize the project by executing Example 10-2. These commands create a Python and Airflow environment in the local directory.

Example 10-2. Initializing the project

```
python -m venv env
astrocloud dev init
```

Then run the commands in Example 10-3 in separate terminals so that you can see the log outputs for each.

Example 10-3. Initializing the project, continued

```
$ cd confluent; docker compose -f docker-compose.yaml up ❶
$ cd marquez/; docker/up.sh --api-port 5002 ❷
$ docker run -it -p 8080:7080 apicurio/apicurio-registry-mem:2.3.0.Final ❸
$ cd control-plane; flask --debug run -p 7000 ❹
$ cd domain-agent; flask --debug run -p 7001 ❺
$ astrocloud dev start ❻
```

❶ Starts the Confluent Platform, which includes Kafka, ZooKeeper, Kafka Connect, REST Proxy, and Schema Registry

❷ Starts Marquez, our OpenLineage service

❸ Starts Apicurio, where AsyncAPI YAML documents for our streaming data products and public schemas get registered

❹ Starts the self-services in the control plane

❺ Starts the domain agents for both the producing and consuming domains

❻ Starts Airflow, which will run any complex workflows in the control plane

Once all of these services are running, we can start iterating through the example.

Installing a Connector

When Confluent Platform starts up, we will need to install a connector that doesn't already exist in the Kafka Connect cluster. Part of our example includes producing dimensional data to join with fact data. This dimensional data will originate from a Postgres database, so we will need a Postgres source connector to ingest data into the Kafka cluster within the domain. The specific Postgres source connector is the Debezium Postgres CDC connector, which reads the Postgres transaction log and captures any events happening to a table, including inserts, updates, and deletes. We will be able to rebuild the exact state of a Postgres table in a materialized view in the streaming platform.

To install the Debezium Postgres connector, domains use the CLI in Example 10-4.

Example 10-4. Installing the Postgres Debezium CDC connector

```
sdm.py connect add debezium/debezium-connector-postgresql:1.9.3
```

The CLI simply calls a Confluent-hosted service to retrieve the connector from Confluent's repository. For environments that don't have access to the internet (implementations that are air gapped), this implementation will need to retrieve the connector from a local repository in the control plane. As you may recall, we've omitted the control-plane repository from this simplified streaming data mesh example.

Part of this service is to also restart the Connect cluster. Restarting (or rebooting) the Connect cluster forces a reload of all the connectors. The Postgres Debezium connector will appear only when the Connect cluster is restarted. The same goes for any other new connector installed.

After installing the connector, you should be able to list it by using the command in Example 10-5. You'll need to ensure that the Connect cluster has fully restarted before requesting this list.

Example 10-5. Listing the available connectors to use in the Connect cluster

```
sdm.py connect plugins |jq
[
  {
    "class": "io.confluent.kafka.connect.datagen.DatagenConnector", ❶
    "type": "source",
    "version": "null"
  },
```

```
{
    "class": "io.debezium.connector.postgresql.PostgresConnector", ❷
    "type": "source",
    "version": "1.9.3.Final"
},
{
    "class": "org.apache.kafka.connect.mirror.MirrorCheckpointConnector",
    "type": "source",
    "version": "1"
},
{
    "class": "org.apache.kafka.connect.mirror.MirrorHeartbeatConnector",
    "type": "source",
    "version": "1"
},
{
    "class": "org.apache.kafka.connect.mirror.MirrorSourceConnector",
    "type": "source",
    "version": "1"
}
]
```

❶ The Datagen connector that will provide clickstream data

❷ The newly installed Debezium Postgres CDC connector

The Confluent Datagen connector will produce mocked-up (fake) clickstream data. This data will serve as our "fact" data. To review, "fact" data is events that occur between entities in DDD. As mentioned earlier, the Postgres database will hold the dimensional data that holds information of the entities in a DDD.

Deploying Clickstream Connector and Auto-Creating Tables

Let's first deploy the Datagen connector to start receiving clickstream data. Example 10-6 shows the command to deploy this connector.

Example 10-6. Deploying a Datagen connector for clickstream data

```
sdm.py connect \
    connector \
    add \ ❶
    clickstream \ ❷
    connect/clickstream.json ❸
```

❶ Instructs the command to deploy a Connector to the connect cluster

❷ The name given to the instance of the connector

❸ The connector's configuration

This command executes these tasks:

1. Sends a request to deploy a Datagen connector
2. Sends a request to Marquez to create the first few nodes in the lineage graph
3. Creates a table-like structure in ksqlDB that references the clickstream data in the topic

Deploy a Datagen connector

The command sends a request to deploy a Datagen connector using the configuration in Example 10-7.

Example 10-7. The configuration for the Datagen clickstream connector

```
{
    "connector.class": "io.confluent.kafka.connect.datagen.DatagenConnector",
    "kafka.topic":"clickstream",
    "max.interval":500,
    "iterations": -1,
    "quickstart":"clickstream"
}
```

You can start consuming the results in a ksqlDB shell (see Example 10-8).

Example 10-8. ksqlDB shell to view the contents of the clickstream topic

```
$ ksql http://localhost:8088
Java HotSpot(TM) 64-Bit Server VM warning: Option UseConcMarkSweepGC was deprecated
in version 9.0 and will likely be removed in a future release.
```

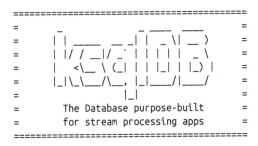

```
Copyright 2017-2021 Confluent Inc.

CLI v7.1.2, Server v7.2.1 located at http://localhost:8088
```

```
WARNING: CLI and server version don't match. This may lead to unexpected errors.
         It is recommended to use a CLI that matches the server version.

Server Status: RUNNING

Having trouble? Type 'help' (case-insensitive) for a rundown of how things work!

ksql> print clickstream;
Key format: HOPPING(JSON) or TUMBLING(JSON) or HOPPING(KAFKA_STRING) or
    TUMBLING(KAFKA_STRING) or KAFKA_STRING
Value format: AVRO
rowtime: 2022/09/21 15:23:25.139 Z, key: [111.90@3328778278569914935/-], value:
    {"ip": "111.90.225.227", "userid": 28, "remote_user": "-", "time": "76841",
    "_time": 76841, "request": "GET /site/login.html HTTP/1.1", "status": "302",
    "bytes": "4096", "referrer": "-", "agent": "Mozilla/5.0 (Windows NT 10.0; Win64;
    x64) AppleWebKit/537.36 (KHTML, like Gecko) Chrome/59.0.3071.115
    Safari/537.36"}, partition: 0 ❶
rowtime: 2022/09/21 15:23:25.373 Z, key: [122.203@3328779382376510518/-], value:
    {"ip": "122.203.236.246", "userid": 38, "remote_user": "-", "time": "76851",
    "_time": 76851, "request": "GET /index.html HTTP/1.1", "status": "200",
    "bytes": "14096", "referrer": "-", "agent": "Mozilla/5.0 (Windows NT 10.0;
    Win64; x64) AppleWebKit/537.36 (KHTML, like Gecko) Chrome/59.0.3071.115
    Safari/537.36"}, partition: 0
rowtime: 2022/09/21 15:23:25.501 Z, key: [222.2@3763089778362169651/-], value:
    {"ip": "222.249.79.93", "userid": 20, "remote_user": "-", "time": "76861",
    "_time": 76861, "request": "GET /images/logo-small.png HTTP/1.1", "status":
    "302", "bytes": "4096", "referrer": "-", "agent": "Mozilla/5.0 (compatible;
    Googlebot/2.1; +http://www.google.com/bot.html)"}, partition: 0
rowtime: 2022/09/21 15:23:25.791 Z, key: [233.245@3328502296856376115/-], value:
    {"ip": "233.245.174.233", "userid": 14, "remote_user": "-", "time": "76871",
    "_time": 76871, "request": "GET /site/user_status.html HTTP/1.1", "status":
    "405", "bytes": "4006", "referrer": "-", "agent": "Mozilla/5.0 (Windows NT
    10.0; Win64; x64) AppleWebKit/537.36 (KHTML, like Gecko) Chrome/59.0.3071.115
    Safari/537.36"}, partition: 0
rowtime: 2022/09/21 15:23:26.232 Z, key: [122.1@3761963882566005812/-], value:
    {"ip": "122.145.8.244", "userid": 10, "remote_user": "-", "time": "76881",
    "_time": 76881, "request": "GET /site/user_status.html HTTP/1.1", "status":
    "200", "bytes": "14096", "referrer": "-", "agent": "Mozilla/5.0 (Windows NT
    10.0; Win64; x64) AppleWebKit/537.36 (KHTML, like Gecko) Chrome/59.0.3071.115
    Safari/537.36"}, partition: 0
^CTopic printing ceased
```

❶ Printing out the contents does not allow users to treat it like a table, where
   you can select, join, and aggregate. We still need to create a ksqlDB table-like
   structure in order to do these table-like functions.

> If the print command doesn't return any records, run this com-
> mand first: SET 'auto.offset.reset'='earliest';. This will
> force the print command to read from the beginning of the topic
> instead of waiting for only new records.

Alternatively, you can use the `kafka-avro-console-consumer` CLI in Example 10-9.

Example 10-9. ksqlDB shell to view the contents of the clickstream topic

```
bin/kafka-avro-console-consumer \
  --bootstrap-server localhost:9092 \
  --topic clickstream
```

Create the first few nodes

The command also sends a request to Marquez to create the first few nodes in the lineage graph. In Figure 10-3, Marquez shows a data set called `datagenconnector.localhost.clickstream` (it is abbreviated in the diagram), which then calls a job named `clickstream.io.confluent.kafka.connect.datagen.DatagenConnector` (also abbreviated), and exposes a data set called `topic.click stream`. The first two nodes are basically the same object since the connector is a data source and a job. The job here is to produce the data set to the third node, `topic.clickstream`, which is a topic in Kafka.

Figure 10-3. Connector section of the lineage graph

Create a table-like structure in ksqlDB

The CLI then creates a table-like structure in ksqlDB that references the clickstream data in the topic. This enables domain engineers to access the contents of the Kafka topic through a SQL interface, allowing them to select, join, and aggregate streaming data. Figure 10-4 expands upon Figure 10-3, appending two additional nodes to the left side of the lineage graph: the first is the job that creates the table-like structure in ksqlDB, and the second is the table-like structure itself as a data set.

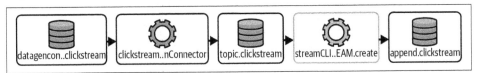

Figure 10-4. Lineage graph showing a job consuming from the topic and creating a table

In Figures 10-3 and 10-4, the cylinders are the data sets, and the gears are the jobs. Data sets are places where data can be accessed like a database, a Kafka topic, or a ksqlDB table. Other examples of data sets are filesystems and message queues. Jobs are processes that move data from one or more data set sources to one or more data set sinks. At this point, domain engineers can just work in ksqlDB to find their data and start building streaming data products.

The output of the `show stream` command now shows the table-like structure, a structure that is read from a Kafka topic of the same name (see Example 10-10).

Example 10-10. Show all the streams currently running in ksqlDB

```
ksql> show streams;

 Stream Name          | Kafka Topic         | Key Format | Value Format | Windowed
----------------------------------------------------------------------------------
 CLICKSTREAM          | clickstream         | KAFKA      | AVRO         | false
 KSQL_PROCESSING_LOG  | default_ksql_proce... | KAFKA    | JSON         | false
----------------------------------------------------------------------------------


ksql> describe clickstream extended;

Name                 : CLICKSTREAM
Type                 : STREAM
Timestamp field      : Not set - using <ROWTIME>
Key format           : KAFKA
Value format         : AVRO
Kafka topic          : clickstream (partitions: 1, replication: 1)
Statement            : CREATE OR REPLACE STREAM CLICKSTREAM (IP STRING, USERID
                       INTEGER, REMOTE_USER STRING, TIME STRING, _TIME BIGINT,
                       REQUEST STRING, STATUS STRING, BYTES STRING, REFERRER STRING,
                       AGENT STRING) WITH (KAFKA_TOPIC='clickstream',
                       KEY_FORMAT='KAFKA', VALUE_FORMAT='AVRO'); ❶

 Field       | Type
------------------------------------
 IP          | VARCHAR(STRING)
 USERID      | INTEGER
 REMOTE_USER | VARCHAR(STRING)
 TIME        | VARCHAR(STRING)
 _TIME       | BIGINT
 REQUEST     | VARCHAR(STRING)
 STATUS      | VARCHAR(STRING)
 BYTES       | VARCHAR(STRING)
 REFERRER    | VARCHAR(STRING)
 AGENT       | VARCHAR(STRING)
------------------------------------

Local runtime statistics
------------------------


(Statistics of the local KSQL server interaction with the Kafka topic clickstream)
ksql>
```

❶ The statement that was executed to create the table-like structure and was registered in OpenLineage.

Deploying the Debezium Postgres CDC Connector

The Confluent *docker-compose.yaml* file contains a Postgres database container that is already enabled for capturing change events. This is a requirement to enable capturing CDC data using the Debezium Postgres connector. The Postgres container in the *docker-compose.yaml* file also has two tables called USERS and PRODUCTS that are pre-populated at startup (see Example 10-11).

Example 10-11. Enabling CDC for a Postgres table

```
create table USERS (
        userid int primary key,
        first_name varchar(63) not null,
        last_name varchar(63) not null,
        phone varchar(63)
);
ALTER TABLE USERS REPLICA IDENTITY FULL; ❶
insert into users values(1, 'foo', 'bar', '123') ❷

create table products (
        productid int primary key,
        name varchar(63) not null,
        description varchar(63)
);
ALTER TABLE products REPLICA IDENTITY FULL; ❸
insert into products values(1, 'p1', 'please buy this, it&#39;s a good product') ❹
```

❶ This statement is required to enable the CDC on the USERS table.

❷ Inserts a record in the USERS table. This record will be captured in the Kafka topic as well as the ksqlDB stream table.

❸ This statement is required to enable the CDC on the PRODUCTS table.

❹ Inserts a record in the PRODUCTS table. This record will be captured in the Kafka topic as well as the ksqlDB stream table.

We will be using the configuration in Example 10-12 when deploying the Debezium Postgres CDC connector. If you study the configuration, notice that the property `table.include.list` contains all the tables from which to capture change events. This means that any insert, update, or delete transactions that get executed on these tables will fire an event that the Debezium Postgres connector will capture and forward to Kafka.

Example 10-12. Configuration for the Debezium Postgres CDC connector

```
{
    "connector.class": "io.debezium.connector.postgresql.PostgresConnector",
    "database.hostname": "postgres",
    "database.port": "5432",
    "database.user": "postgres",
    "database.password": "postgres",
    "database.dbname" : "postgres",
    "plugin.name": "pgoutput",
    "slot.name": "pgoutput_sdm",
    "snapshot.mode": "always",
    "database.server.name": "postgres",
    "database.history.kafka.bootstrap.servers": "broker:9092",
    "database.history.kafka.topic": "pg-schemas",
    "table.include.list": "public.users,public.products",  ❶
    "transforms": "route",
    "transforms.route.type": "org.apache.kafka.connect.transforms.RegexRouter",
    "transforms.route.regex": "([^.]+)\\.([^.]+)\\.([^.]+)",
    "transforms.route.replacement": "$3"
}
```

❶ This property specifies the tables to include when the Debezium connector reads the write-ahead log (WAL). The WAL captures all the change events for the tables that were configured for CDC in Example 10-11. In this case, there are two tables: USERS and PRODUCTS.

In Example 10-13 the CLI is used to deploy the Debezium Postgres CDC connector into the Connect cluster. The connecter is also configured to capture change events from two tables: USERS and PRODUCTS.

Example 10-13. Deploy the Debezium Postgres CDC connector

```
sdm.py connect connector add users connect/debezium.json
```

The resulting lineage graph shows two tables from Postgres being consumed by a Debezium connector. The data for each table gets written into the corresponding Kafka topics and table-like structures in ksqlDB (see Figure 10-5). The configuration can be changed to add more tables, which will result in more data sets being connected to the Debezium Job in the lineage graph.

We can now enrich this real-time data by using stream joins.

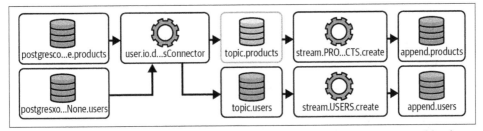

Figure 10-5. Lineage graph showing the Debezium connector consuming two tables from Postgres and automatically creating two tables

Enrichment of Streaming Data

Until now, we have not yet decided what our streaming data product will be. We simply started ingesting our data into ksqlDB. We've created a data platform that can allow us to experiment on building data products.

We have three data sets streaming into Kafka and into ksqlDB: clickstream, users, and products. Example 10-14 describes USERS and CLICKSTREAM in ksqlDB. We can join them together but need to transform the USERS stream.

Example 10-14. Table and stream descriptions

```
ksql> describe users;
Name : USERS
 Field      | Type
--------------------------------------------
 BEFORE     | STRUCT< ❶
                USERID INTEGER,
                FIRST_NAME VARCHAR(STRING),
                LAST_NAME VARCHAR(STRING),
                PHONE VARCHAR(STRING)
              >

 AFTER      | STRUCT< ❷
                USERID INTEGER, ❸
                FIRST_NAME VARCHAR(STRING),
                LAST_NAME VARCHAR(STRING),
                PHONE VARCHAR(STRING)
              >

 SOURCE     | STRUCT<
                VERSION VARCHAR(STRING),
                CONNECTOR VARCHAR(STRING),
                NAME VARCHAR(STRING),
                TS_MS BIGINT,
                SNAPSHOT VARCHAR(STRING),
                DB VARCHAR(STRING),
                SEQUENCE VARCHAR(STRING),
```

```
                    SCHEMA VARCHAR(STRING),
                    TABLE VARCHAR(STRING),
                    TXID BIGINT,
                    LSN BIGINT,
                    XMIN BIGINT
                    >
OP            | VARCHAR(STRING)
TS_MS         | BIGINT
TRANSACTION   | STRUCT<
                    ID VARCHAR(STRING),
                    TOTAL_ORDER BIGINT,
                    DATA_COLLECTION_ORDER BIGINT
                    >
-------------------------------------------------

ksql> describe clickstream;

Name    : CLICKSTREAM
 Field        | Type
-------------------------------------
 IP           | VARCHAR(STRING)
 USERID       | INTEGER    ❹
 REMOTE_USER  | VARCHAR(STRING)
 TIME         | VARCHAR(STRING)
 _TIME        | BIGINT
 REQUEST      | VARCHAR(STRING)
 STATUS       | VARCHAR(STRING)
 BYTES        | VARCHAR(STRING)
 REFERRER     | VARCHAR(STRING)
 AGENT        | VARCHAR(STRING)
-------------------------------------
```

❶ The BEFORE state of a record in the Debezium CDC format.

❷ The AFTER state of a record in the Debezium CDC format.

❸ The USER table has a USERID field that we can join with the CLICKSTREAM stream.

❹ The CLICKSTREAM table has a USERID field that we can join with the USERS table.

Since CLICKSTREAM has a field that identifies users, USERS can be joined to CLICKSTREAM, creating a streaming data product that provides clickstream data enriched with user data to other domains.

The structure of the USERS table in Example 10-14 is a complex Debezium format that shows a lot of the metadata that is part of the change event. The BEFORE and AFTER fields correspond to the before and after state of the record after the change was made. We will not be using the other fields in the Debezium format: SOURCE, OP, TS_MS, and TRANSACTION. They are well documented on the Debezium website (*https://debezium.io*).

USERS and CLICKSTREAM are different table-like structures. CLICKSTREAM is called a *stream*, and the USERS structure is called a *table*. To join CLICKSTREAM and USERS, we need to better understand the differences between these structures.

Stream versus table

In ksqlDB, a *stream* is a table-like structure that is made up of discrete events. In Chapter 4 we talked about the differences between fact and dimensional data. ksqlDB streams tend to hold fact data.

Alternatively, in ksqlDB, a *table* is a table-like structure that is made up of changes to records. We also talked about change data capture data (CDC) in Chapter 4. These are change events that have occurred in a database table. These events include inserts, updates, and deletes. CDC data tends to live in ksqlDB tables where these changes are materialized into a view (or just *materialized view*) that resembles the current state of the database table from which the CDC data originated.

Another way to think about this is that ksqlDB streams (streams created from ksqlDB with transformed and/or enriched data) contain only insert events, while ksqlDB tables contain inserts, updates, and deletes. ksqlDB streams are very easy to understand because events just get inserted (or appended) to the end of the stream. ksqlDB tables (materialized views) need to be built.

In ksqlDB, tables need to be created from ksqlDB streams. Example 10-15 shows how the USERS table creates a table called USERS_MATERIALIZED_VIEW. This will create the exact state as the original database table in ksqlDB.

Example 10-15. Creating a materialized view from a stream

```
CREATE TABLE USERS_MATERIALIZED_VIEW AS ❶
  select
    after->userid,
    LATEST_BY_OFFSET(after->first_name), ❷
    LATEST_BY_OFFSET(after->last_name),
    LATEST_BY_OFFSET(after->phone)
  from USERS
  GROUP BY after->userid ❸
  EMIT CHANGES; ❹
```

❶ Create Table As Select (also known as CTAS) creates a materialized view from a stream.

❷ The function LATEST_BY_OFFSET() gets the latest version of the field that will be in the latest offset in the Kafka topic partition. Executing this function to all of the fields provides the latest state of all records.

❸ Grouping by userid will create the record's latest state by its user ID.

❹ EMIT CHANGES tells ksqlDB to continue to push changes to the ksqlDB table as new change events arrive.

As you see when we use the describe command on the USERS_MATERIALIZED_VIEW table in Example 10-16, it can be joined on USERID with the CLICKSTREAM data.

Example 10-16. Describing a materialized view

```
ksql> describe USERS_MATERIALIZED_VIEW;

Name                    : USERS_MATERIALIZED
 Field      | Type
-------------------------------------------------
 USERID     | INTEGER          (primary key)
 FIRST_NAME | VARCHAR(STRING)
 LAST_NAME  | VARCHAR(STRING)
 PHONE      | VARCHAR(STRING)
-------------------------------------------------
```

Example 10-17 joins CLICKSTREAM with USERS_MATERIALIZED_VIEW, enriching the clickstream with user data.

Example 10-17. Enriching the clickstream with user information

```
CREATE OR REPLACE STREAM CLICK_USERS AS
select
  c.ip,
  c.userid userid,
  c.agent agent,
  c.request request,
  c.status status,
  u.first_name first_name,
  u.last_name last_name,
  u.phone phone
from clickstream c
join USERS_MATERIALIZED u on c.userid = u.userid
EMIT CHANGES
```

Each ksqlDB statement that is used will need to be deployed using the CLI so that the statement can be registered as a job within the streaming data mesh. Figure 10-6 shows the OpenLineage graph that we have built so far. It illustrates consuming from the original sources to the data set that has enriched clickstream data.

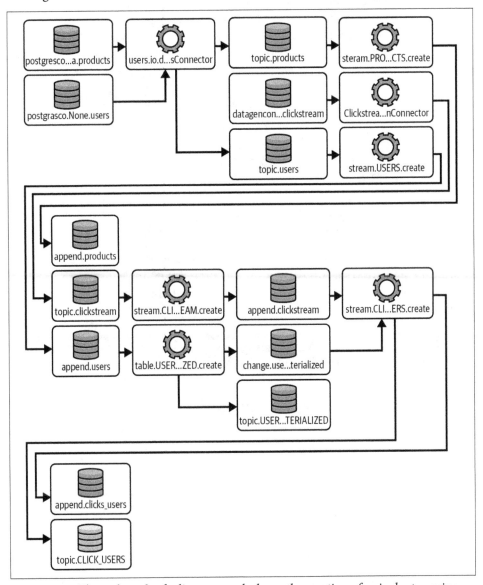

Figure 10-6. The end result of a lineage graph shows the creation of a single streaming data product

At this point, the domain product owner can decide that we have a streaming data product. The next step is to publish the product so that others can discover, request access, and consume from it.

Publishing the Data Product

To publish the streaming data product, you need to execute the command in Example 10-18. This command will obtain the Kafka topic that backs the ksqlDB table. All ksqlDB tables and streams are backed by a Kafka topic. The command will construct an AsyncAPI YAML document and then push the YAML document to Apicurio.

Example 10-18. Enriching the clickstream with user information

```
$ sdm.py streaming publish --help

Usage: sdm.py streaming publish [OPTIONS] STREAM_NAME
Publishes an append/change stream or stream/table as a streaming data product

╭─ Arguments ──────────────────────────────────────────────╮
│ *    stream_name      TEXT  [default: None] [required] │
╰──────────────────────────────────────────────────────────╯
```

The result of this command creates an entry in Apicurio. It takes the user's domain information and creates a GROUP within Apicurio. For example, in Figure 10-7, the group name is "east," which is the name of the domain publishing this streaming data product.

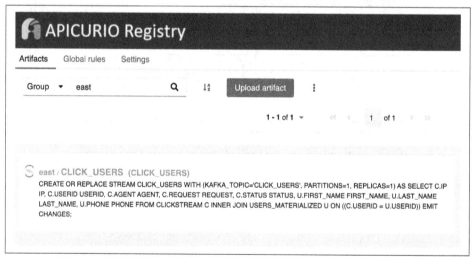

Figure 10-7. Apicurio showing the group name that corresponds to the domain that produced the streaming data product

Notice also that the description of the streaming data product shows the SQL that populates the Kafka topic.

Apicurio also automatically generates the API page that shows the schema of the data as well as an example payload (see Figure 10-8). As you may recall in Chapter 4, we generated the HTML for this API page by using a command-line tool.

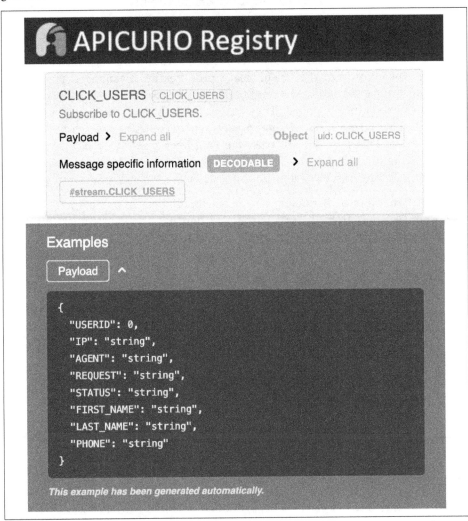

Figure 10-8. Apicurio automatically generates an API page complete with payload. We did this ourselves from the command line in Chapter 4.

Now that our streaming data product has been published, other domains can request access and subscribe to it.

Consuming Streaming Data Products

Through Apicurio, consumers can now search and discover streaming data products. We've published only one streaming data product, so searching for it is easy.

In the Documentation tab of a streaming data product in Apicurio, an HTML page was generated from the AsyncAPI YAML document. We added a tag called #lineage that takes you directly to the OpenLineage page for the streaming data product. Consumers can see the entire lineage and feel confident that the product was derived from the source(s) they expected. They can also step through the lineage to ensure that the data has been processed appropriately and complies to any security policies or regulations. This provides the trust the consumer needs to decide to use the streaming data product. Let's assume that streaming data product provides enough information for the consuming domain to subscribe to the data product.

To get started, we switch domains by using the CLI in Example 10-19. In this case, we're switching from the east to the west domain. The west domain wants to subscribe to the CLICK_USERS streaming data product.

Example 10-19. Switching domains

```
$ sdm.py switch-domain --help

 Usage: sdm.py switch-domain [OPTIONS] DOMAIN


╭─ Arguments ─────────────────────────────────────────────╮
│ *    domain      TEXT  [default: None] [required]       │
╰─────────────────────────────────────────────────────────╯
╭─ Options ───────────────────────────────────────────────╮
│ --help             Show this message and exit.          │
╰─────────────────────────────────────────────────────────╯

# Example
$ sdm.py switch-domain west
```

In Apicurio, there's an assigned Global or Content ID (see Figure 10-9). Logged in to the CLI as the west domain, we will use this ID to request access to the streaming data product produced from the east domain.

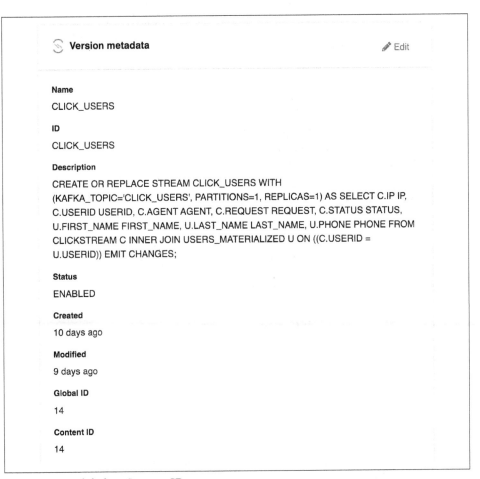

Version metadata   ✎ Edit

Name
CLICK_USERS

ID
CLICK_USERS

Description
CREATE OR REPLACE STREAM CLICK_USERS WITH
(KAFKA_TOPIC='CLICK_USERS', PARTITIONS=1, REPLICAS=1) AS SELECT C.IP IP,
C.USERID USERID, C.AGENT AGENT, C.REQUEST REQUEST, C.STATUS STATUS,
U.FIRST_NAME FIRST_NAME, U.LAST_NAME LAST_NAME, U.PHONE PHONE FROM
CLICKSTREAM C INNER JOIN USERS_MATERIALIZED U ON ((C.USERID =
U.USERID)) EMIT CHANGES;

Status
ENABLED

Created
10 days ago

Modified
9 days ago

Global ID
14

Content ID
14

Figure 10-9. Global or Content ID

Example 10-20 shows how the consuming domain will request access to a streaming
data product. All requests for access to streaming data products are put into a
database for approval by the owning domain.

Example 10-20. Switching domains

```
$ sdm.py domain request --help

Usage: sdm.py domain request [OPTIONS] DOMAIN_ID DATA_PRODUCT_ID

Requests access to a data product by the current (your) domain.

╭─ Arguments ─────────────────────────────────────────────╮
│ *    domain_id        TEXT  [default: None] [required] │
╰─────────────────────────────────────────────────────────╯
```

```
╭─ Options ─────────────────────────────────────────────────╮
│ --help                Show this message and exit.          │
╰───────────────────────────────────────────────────────────╯
```

```
# Example
$ sdm.py domain request east CLICK_USERS
```

Example 10-21 shows the command the data product owner in the origin domain would execute to grant access to the consuming domain. The implementation of this will trigger a request to create a cluster link between the two domains.

Example 10-21. Granting access to a streaming data product

```
$ sdm.py dp access grant --help

Usage: sdm.py dp access grant [OPTIONS] DATA_PRODUCT_ID CONSUMING_DOMAIN

Grants (removes) access to a data product to a consuming domain.
╭─ Arguments ───────────────────────────────────────────────╮
│ *    data_product_id     TEXT  [default: None] [required] │
│ *    consuming_domain    TEXT  [default: None] [required] │
╰───────────────────────────────────────────────────────────╯
╭─ Options ─────────────────────────────────────────────────╮
│ --remove      --no-remove    [default: no-remove]          │
│ --help                       Show this message and exit.   │
╰───────────────────────────────────────────────────────────╯
```

```
# Example
$ sdm.py dp access grant west 14 ❶
```

❶ Here the origin domain grants to the west domain streaming data product 14, the ID provided by Apicurio.

Triggering the creation of a cluster link between domains is handled by an Airflow DAG. This DAG subscribes consumers to newly granted streaming data products, allowing access to the subscriber. Triggering an Airflow DAG can be done by starting the workflow with an Airflow sensor that waits for events to happen. The sensor used in our example is a SimpleHttpOperator that polls an HTTP endpoint until a successful response is received. Other Airflow sensors can be used, like BashSensor, PythonSensor, or SqlSensor. All Airflow sensors basically check for something to happen before executing.

The DAG provides a way to orchestrate the workflow that builds a cluster link between two domains that can be easily modified and visualized. It's important to understand that workflow orchestration tools like Airflow are used here to allow for quick and agile modifications to adapt to changing regulations and easy auditing.

Ultimately, the end goal for the Airflow DAG is to interact with the domain agent to execute the creation of the cluster link that will link streaming data products from the producing domain to the consuming domain. In this on-premises version of a streaming data mesh, the domain agent will be handled by the REST Proxy server that comes with Confluent Platform.

To recap, Figure 10-10 shows a local schema registry for each domain. This allows each domain to manage its own schemas so that they are not exposed to the other domains in the mesh.

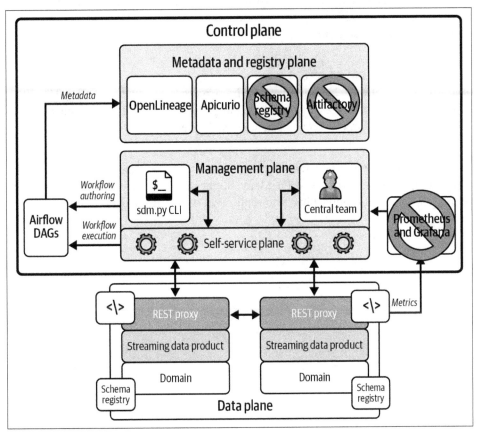

Figure 10-10. REST Proxy and local schema registry

Through this isolation, domains now have autonomy in defining and evolving their schemas. Again, the schema registry in the control plane will be handled by Apicurio, which will handle the evolution of the streaming data product once it is published. Apicurio protects the consuming domains from breaking schema changes.

Also in Figure 10-10, the REST Proxy takes on the role of the domain agent. The REST Proxy controls the cluster links between the domains.

When the Airflow DAG completes the cluster link via the REST Proxy, a topic appears in the consuming domain's Kafka cluster. This allows the topic to consume the streaming data products locally. Again, the replication of the data from source Kafka to destination Kafka is handled by the cluster link and is completely hidden from either domain.

Consuming domains can now start processing the streaming data product for which they have been granted access—the same data that originated from the transactional database. This process of building, publishing, and granting is repeated for all streaming data products.

A lot of full-time employees (FTEs) are needed to manage this on-premises version of a streaming data mesh. This may require a reorganization of existing FTEs into new roles that are created by the data mesh implementation within the control plane. Alternatively, a streaming data mesh can be implemented more easily with fully managed SaaS providers.

The OpenLineage graph generated from source data to destination domain can get really complex (see Figure 10-11). Many of the fully managed SaaS services can simplify development, publishing, and replication of streaming data products.

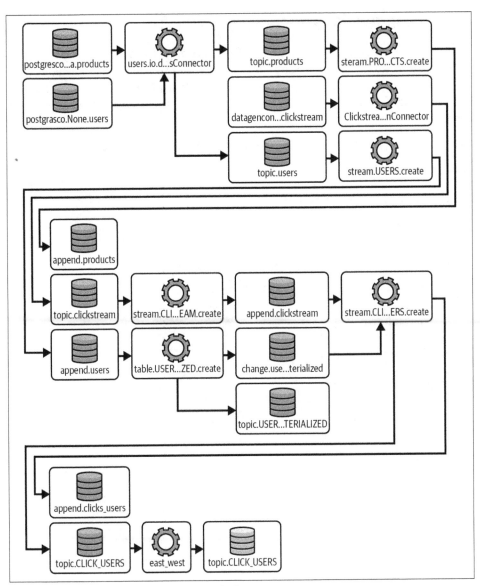

Figure 10-11. OpenLineage with cluster link

Fully Managed SaaS Services

As of the writing of this book, there isn't a SaaS version of the control plane described in this chapter. You will be required to assemble the control plane by aggregating many SaaS services. Some components of the control plane will also still need to be self-managed because the SaaS company that backs those components doesn't yet exist, or exists only in stealth mode.

Here is a list of some of the most popular fully managed SaaS services you can use:

Streaming platforms:

- Confluent Cloud managed Kafka
- Redpanda fully managed data
- StreamNative fully managed Apache Pulsar
- DataStax Astra streaming fully managed Apache Pulsar
- Amazon Managed Streaming for Apache Kafka (MSK)
- Aiven managed Kafka
- Instaclustr managed Kafka
- Red Hat managed Kafka

Stream processing platforms:

- Decodable
- DeltaStream
- Popsink
- ksqlDB
- Materialized
- RisingWave
- Timeplus

Metadata platforms:

- Confluent Schema Registry
- Aiven schema registry
- Red Hat Service registry

Connectors:

- Confluent
- Red Hat
- Aiven

Unfortunately, the service that we still need to manage is Marquez for the OpenLineage service. Also, it may be necessary to self-manage an Apicurio server that can accept an AsyncAPI document and act as a temporary streaming data catalog. As of the writing of this book, some fully managed data catalogs are available—none of the existing implementations address the needs of streaming data.

Implementing a streaming data mesh using fully managed services is very much like implementing a streaming data mesh on premises. The advantage of using fully managed services is that the responsibility for SLAs, uptime, and scaling is now placed on the streaming provider. Another benefit is the simplification of building streaming data products. For example, when using a SaaS streaming platform, you can simplify the creation of a lot of your streaming data products by reducing the steps to create them.

To do the SaaS version of a streaming data mesh, a new CLI that supports the cloud SaaS services you'll be using needs to be built. In our example, we will be using Apache Pulsar as the streaming platform and a SaaS streaming platform.

Both of these SaaS services come with their own CLIs that operations to their services and security require. This can reduce the effort of building our cloud streaming data mesh CLI in half.

Example 10-22 shows how to install both of the CLIs on Apple-based computers.

Example 10-22. Installing CLIs on Apple

```
$ brew tap streamnative/streamnative ❶
$ brew install pulsarctl

$ curl -L releases.decodable.co/install | bash ❷
```

❶ Installs the StreamNative Pulsar CLI

❷ Installs the Decodable CLI

Installation of these CLIs will differ on Linux and Windows platforms. The documentation for Pulsar (*https://oreil.ly/Qr3WP*) and Decodable (*https://oreil.ly/c_Dff*) provide instructions on how to install for your specific platform.

The command in Example 10-23 creates a stream and connection. To review, a stream is a table-like structure that holds streaming data. In this case, we are going to capture change events (CDCs) from the users table in a Postgres database and write them into a stream with the same name.

Example 10-23. Deploying a Datagen connector for clickstream data

```
sdmc.py connect \
    connector \
    add \ ❶
    users \ ❷
    schema/users.json ❸
    connect/postgres-cdc.json ❹
```

❶ Instructs the command to deploy a connector to the connect cluster

❷ The name given to the instance of the connector

❸ The schema for the stream the data will write to

❹ The connector's configuration

This command also automatically creates the OpenLineage graph that shows consuming from the users table from Postgres and immediately creating a materialized view. It's a three-node graph, compared to a five-node graph that is created in an on-premises version. Similarly, we can create a Datagen connector in fewer lineage nodes (see Figure 10-12).

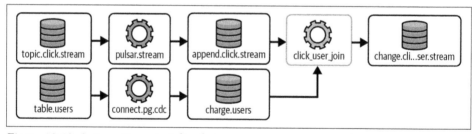

Figure 10-12. Automatic materialized view

The architecture we're building is slightly different from the architecture we've seen in previous chapters. In Figure 10-13, we are using a SaaS stream processor to perform SQL transformations on streaming data in order to create our data products as well as replication of streaming data products between domains.

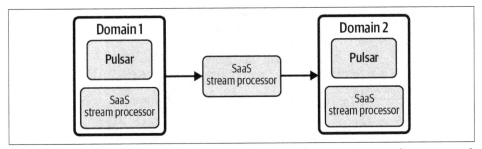

Figure 10-13. A SaaS stream processor using Apache Pulsar for SQL transformation and replication between domains

The SaaS stream processor allows us to be streaming-platform agnostic. This allows domains to be autonomous by using the streaming platform of their choice. In Figure 10-14, we can replace Apache Pulsar with Redpanda at the source domain and Kafka at the destination domain. The SaaS stream processor also allows for other streaming platforms (such as Amazon Kinesis). This is unlike ksqlDB, which requires streaming platforms that support offsets like Kafka and Redpanda. Confluent's cluster-linking feature is dependent on its version of Kafka and cannot be used in other streaming implementations.

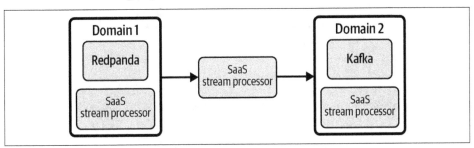

Figure 10-14. Redpanda to a SaaS stream processor replication with a SaaS stream processor

Adding a SaaS stream processor into the solution does not change the overall architecture. It only simplifies streaming data product development and publishing. As shown in Figure 10-15, it does so by reducing the number of "hops" it takes to reach the consuming domain.

All the commands needed to get from data product derivatives to consuming data products from the destination domain are nearly the same. Their differences are subtle and negligible. Again in Figure 10-16, there are fewer nodes to get the streaming data product to the destination domain.

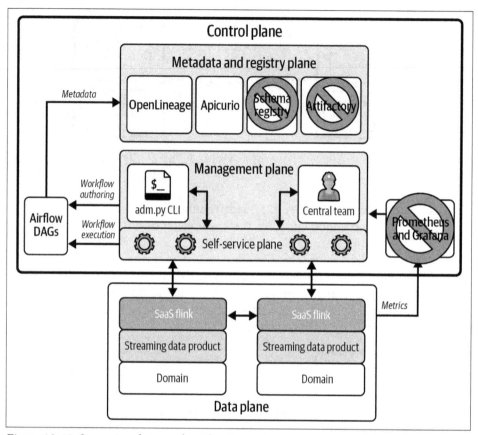

Figure 10-15. Streaming data mesh with a SaaS stream processor and data plane replicator

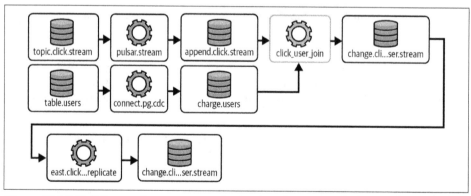

Figure 10-16. Full lineage from source to destination domain, including replication of streaming data product

Whether you are building a streaming data mesh on premises or on the cloud, the experience in implementing, publishing, and consuming data products is the same.

Summary and Considerations

Here are some things you should consider when building a streaming data mesh:

- The strictness of your security will dictate the amount of difficulty in implementing streaming data mesh.

- Building a cloud streaming data mesh could simplify implementation from the standpoint that many components of the mesh are deployable as SaaS. Security, however, will add to the complexity and difficulty—especially when indentity services, private networks, and hybrid architectures are required.

- OpenLineage schema specification does not support complex data sets as of the writing this book. You will need to rely on Apicurio to accurately describe your schemas.

- Having lots of services will require timing considerations when calling their self-service APIs. For example, the schema registry may not have schema soon enough for you to use it in your next line of code in your CLI. Consider adding timeouts or callbacks when aggregating services into one CLI command.

- Airflow DAGs are better when the workflow requires inputs from multiple domains and control planes. It is also important to document these DAGs to avoid unnecessary and redundant Airflow DAGs when implementing a streaming data mesh.

- Some implementors may consider using microservices in a *saga* pattern when implementing a workflow instead of using Airflow DAGs. This is doable, but understand you may not be able to be agile enough to make changes to continuously changing regulations and policies. Each microservice will have a separate software development lifecycle, while an Airflow DAG is a single deployment.

- Choose applications to run in the control plane that already have a well-defined API for clients to use. Coupled with Airflow, these applications will cover most of the self-services needed to implement an easy-to-use streaming data mesh. This will reduce the number of self-services you actually have to implement.

Ultimately, building a streaming data mesh can be easy because most of the hard components are already built for you. The only requirement is to aggregate and integrate these components as self-services for domains to use. At the end, it's all about making the tasks for domains work with data and metadata without requiring super-specialized skills. A knowledge of streaming and SQL is the main requirement.

Good luck and don't mess your mesh up!

Index

enriching streaming data, 183-187
fully managed SaaS services, 196-201
getting started, 170
installing connectors, 175
overview of, 169
publishing data products, 188
scenario for, 171
streaming data products (see data products)
streams, versus tables, 185
Structured Query Language (SQL), 57-62
subdata mesh, 30
subdomains, 30
supplemental material, obtaining, ix
Swagger, 70
synchronous data sources, 52

T

table-like structures, 179, 185
task-level resource charge-backs, 40
throughput tags, 84
tiered storage, 23-25
timeouts, 201
tokenization, 118
tools and platforms
    Apache Spark, 43
    data governance, 103
    for domain ownership, 39
    fully managed SaaS services, 196-201
    SaaS stream processors, 125
    stream processing engines, 127
topic command, 108
topic-related commands, 109
traditional views, 67
training-serving skew, 16

U

ubiquitous language, in domain-driven design,
    37

udf command, 112-114
UDFs (see user-defined functions)
update command
    UDFs to newer versions, 113
    updates connectors to newer versions, 112
    updates/replaces deployed sqls, 113
usage statistics, 98
usage-based charge-backs, 40
user-defined functions (UDFs)
    encryption and decryption UDFs, 118
    tokenization and detokenization UDFs, 118
    updating to newer versions, 113

V

validation rules, 122
versioning, 85
virtual private cloud (VPC), 174

W

workflow orchestration, 144-147

Y

YAML documents (AsyncAPI)
    building, 72
    channels and topic section, 75
    components section, 76
    generating data product pages, 98-101
    messages section, 77
    objects asyncapi, externalDocs, info, and
        tags, 72
    schemas subsection, 78
    security schemes sections, 80
    servers and security section, 74
    traits section, 81

Z

ZD (see Dehghani, Zhamak)

About the Authors

Hubert Dulay is a developer relations and data engineer at StarTree. He is a veteran engineer with over 20 years of experience in big and fast data and MLOps. Hubert has compiled his experiences with data from his time while consulting for many financial institutions, health-care organizations, and telecommunications companies, providing simple solutions that solved many data problems.

Stephen Mooney is an independent data scientist and data engineer serving multiple clients. With over 20 years of experience in big data, MLOps, and data science, he has worked in many major companies across health care, retail, and the public sector. Through this experience, Stephen has delivered many technical and functional projects throughout the entire product lifecycle.

Colophon

The animal on the cover of *Streaming Data Mesh* is a walleye (*Sander vitreus*), a freshwater fish native to Canada and the northern United States.

The name "walleye" comes from their eyes, which appear opaque because of a reflective pigment called the *tapetrum lucidum*. This allows walleyes to see well in low lighting or rough water. As a result, they tend to feed at night or in choppy water, using their eyesight as an advantage over their prey. Walleyes feed on other fish, such as yellow perch, crayfish, and minnows, and have taste buds in their lips.

In appearance, walleyes are mostly olive and gold in color with a white belly. They can grow up to 31 inches and 20 pounds. Their lifespan is generally 10 to 20 years, although the oldest recorded lifespan is 29 years. Fishing plays a part in their average lifespan, as walleyes are popular among anglers. Walleye fishing is regulated for population control, and walleye hatcheries help with restocking lakes and rivers.

Hatcheries also help with another problem: cross-breeding. Hatcheries ensure purebred walleye, whereas in nature, walleyes sometimes cross-breed with sauger, producing "saugeye." Female walleye typically lay up to 500,000 eggs. The eggs are laid on or between rocks, with an incubation period of about two weeks, and neither parent tends to the eggs.

The current IUCN conservation status of the walleye is Least Concern. Many of the animals on O'Reilly covers are endangered; all of them are important to the world.

The cover illustration is by Karen Montgomery, based on an antique line engraving from *Dover*. The cover fonts are Gilroy Semibold and Guardian Sans. The text font is Adobe Minion Pro; the heading font is Adobe Myriad Condensed; and the code font is Dalton Maag's Ubuntu Mono.

O'REILLY®

Learn from experts.
Become one yourself.

Books | Live online courses
Instant Answers | Virtual events
Videos | Interactive learning

Get started at oreilly.com.

Printed in the USA
CPSIA information can be obtained
at www.ICGtesting.com
JSHW060951260324
59876JS00010B/287

9 781098 130725